AFTERNOON DELIGHT

Why Soaps Still Matter

AFTERNOON DELIGHT

Why Soaps Still Matter

CAROLYN HINSEY

4th STREET
MEDIA

Cover Design by: Luke Pidgeon

Printed in the United States of America

ISBN: 978-0-9844406-3-4

4th Street Media, LLC
406 Broadway, Suite 220C
Santa Monica, CA 90401
www.4thstreetmedia.com

For my friend Frank

And every soap fan who ever "tuned in tomorrow."

Acknowledgments

This book was a complete labor of love because I love soap operas. I love the people who watch them, and I love the people who work on them. I especially appreciate the help of my many soap pals who let me interview them, helped refresh my memory, or even just gave me permission to tell a "forbidden" story.

Thank you Scott Barton, Mark Teschner, Rena Sofer, Martha Byrne, Hunt Block, Sonia Blangiardo, Shawn Dudley, Thorsten Kaye, Michelle Stafford and Frank Valentini, for helping me tap into the amazing energy I have been privileged to see firsthand working in daytime for 20 years. Special thanks to Thorsten and Michelle for talking me through the craziness at the end when two soaps got canceled as this book went to print.

Thanks to my publisher Brian Howie at 4th Street Media for writing on my Facebook page, "Happy Birthday. Now let me publish your book" and then actually doing it.

Thanks also for the title and cover concept. Please continue to tell people that is my cleavage. Thanks to Shelli Stutz at 4th Street Media for being so enthusiastic with this project, even though the closest she ever got to a soap was "Beverly Hills, 90210." I'll take it!

Thanks to Lynn Leahey and Stephanie Sloane at *Soap Opera Digest* for editing my copy (and me) perfectly for 19 years; making every day fun even when we had our own little soap operas going on, and for letting me curl my hair at work. Thanks also to photo editor Bryan Beckley who steered me through the dusty photo files for the gems found here. Thanks to *TV Guide* Columnist Michael Logan for making me appear smarter, better and funnier in all of our columns and conversations together - even when we WILDLY disagreed. ("Passions," anyone?)

Thank you to John Paschal, Ruby Montgomery and everyone at JPI Photos for the invaluable assistance with most of the photos in this book. Your enthusiasm, talent and professionalism explains why you are #1 in the business.

Thank you to Dallas Mayr (aka famed horror writer Jack Ketchum) for being such a good, daily friend, and for feigning interest in soaps so convincingly. Dallas steered me to his fellow horror writer and friend Peter Straub, a devoted "One Life To Live" fan, who offers the most poetic description of why soaps matter in this entire book. Thank you, Peter, from my daytime and "nighttime" self.

Thank you to my late grandmother Sarah Callen Hinsey for teaching me the great value in continuing drama as we watched "As The World Turns" together. And thank you to my parents Phyllis and Joe Hinsey for forbidding me to watch soap operas, which made me want to watch them more. To their credit, my mom and dad supported my passion even though the only television they have watched to this day is news and sports.

Thank you to my sister Sara for offering to line edit this book, and for letting me fill up her DVR with soaps every time I visit, and to Heather McDonald for her constant support and party-throwing magic. Thank you to all my Pi Phis at Indiana for making it cool to watch soaps, and for updating me on what I missed when my Journalism classes got in the way of Luke and Laura on the run. I am so grateful for our time together in that big white house, and for all the crazy times since. Thank you to Patty McGreevey for letting us turn her bar, Blondies, into a Soap Opera Clubhouse for charity events - raising almost $100,000 over the years.

Thank you to my *New York Daily News* pals for teaching me how to write well on deadline – and for letting me into the club.

And thanks to my dear friends Cat McKenzie, Jeanne Blake and Cynthia Germanotta, who read various parts of this book and offered excellent insight and comments. A special thanks to Cynthia who made notes for me, crystallized my chapters, and helped hone my thoughts. Everyone should have a supportive friend like Cynthia - especially soap characters. If they did, there'd be a lot fewer loony bins on daytime.

But most of all thank you to the thousands of passionate, kooky, rabid, funny, opinionated, SMART soap fans I have had the pleasure to get to know at events, via email or via Facebook over the 20 years I have been writing about soaps.

We were right, you know.

Contents

AFTERNOON DELIGHT

Why Soaps Still Matter

I had strep throat as a wee tot so I was home from school for a week lying in bed. I started watching "All My Children" and I thought, "This is interesting." Then I saw "Ryan's Hope" and I thought, "I'll give this one a try." Frank Ryan fell down a flight of stairs and I was totally hooked. I hooked my sister and then my cousin stayed with us one summer and we completely hooked her.

About a year later I was sick again, so I thought I'm going to give all of them a try. I watched "One Life To Live" and there was a story with Tina Lord that I thought was awesome. Then "General Hospital" came on and Luke and Laura were hiding out in the department store.

I faked being sick to watch sometimes. I was completely hooked to all of them for different reasons, but as time went on I became more hooked on "GH." One time, my sister and I missed the bus so we ran home from school and got home just in time to watch it. We were completely in love with Tony Geary. We weren't crazy people who just knew him as Luke, we could separate him as being a great actor.

Cut to 2004, when I won an Emmy the same year Tony Geary won. It was extremely profound for me, because he is one of the reasons I am an actress today. Part of the reason I decided to do what I do is because soaps made me see more than just the characters; they made me look at different aspects of life.

That's what good soaps do.

- Michelle Stafford from Los Angeles

OPENING SCENE: CUE THE INTRO MUSIC

On November 16, 1981, 50 women snuck out of their offices at the Chicago Tribune and skulked down to the cafeteria to watch Luke and Laura's wedding on "General Hospital."

I know, because I was one of them. I had just graduated from college, and it was my first day of work at my first real job. Thirty million other people across America did the same, making the November 16th and 17th episodes of GH the most-watched in soap opera history.

What made so many people tune in? Many were curious to see movie star (and confessed "General Hospital" fan) Elizabeth Taylor guest star as the evil Helena Cassadine. "My curse on you Laura and Luke," Helena hissed from the shadows as the bride and groom cut the wedding cake. "My curse on both of you!" Some watched because they had seen Anthony Geary (Luke) and Genie Francis (Laura) on a recent cover of *Newsweek* magazine. Even before the Internet there was still buzz.

But true "General Hospital" fans (like me) ditched work and tuned in because this was the culmination of one of the most dramatic and controversial love stories ever told on daytime. A love story that began with Luke raping Laura on a disco floor - later re-termed a "seduction" when "General Hospital" realized how popular Geary had become - and ended two years later at the altar.

"I Lucas Lorenzo Spencer take you Laura Webber Baldwin..."

Laura beamed and fans swooned, transfixed by the pink bridesmaid dresses, the giant wedding cake, and the sunny LA location shoot that doubled for the Port Charles Mayor's Mansion where clearly no expense had been spared. "No more worrying about Laura," sighed her relieved father, Rick, at the reception. "No, Luke will keep her safe," smiled her mom, Lesley. Ha! Laura threw her bouquet, her ex-husband Scotty Baldwin crashed the wedding and caught it, Scotty and Luke had a bloody fight ("I'll kill you!" screamed Luke) and the bride started sobbing. Ah, soap operas!

The biggest reason so many people "attended" Luke and Laura's wedding was because back in 1981, you had to actually *watch* a show to see what happened. (There were no DVRs, and VCRs were just being invented.) There were only three national networks - ABC, CBS and NBC - so there was little competition. Of course there are 700 more channels today, but to put GH's 30 million wedding viewers in perspective, the 2010 finale of "American Idol" - which was Simon Cowell's farewell episode, garnered 24.2 million people. The 2010 World Series averaged 14.3 million viewers. So it's no wonder Luke and Laura's wedding is considered the pinnacle of soap operas; indeed, all of daytime television.

A lot has changed since then – we'll get to that - but soap operas remain a unique daytime destination. Game shows, talk shows, judge shows and reality shows have flooded the airwaves and fractured viewer interest, but soaps still shine like the back-from-the-dead, wedding interrupting, vixen-loving, DNA tested, beacon they are. Besides, as powerhouses Oprah Winfrey and Regis Philbin exit Daytime in 2011, soaps are left as the only thing separating ABC, CBS and NBC from those 700 cable channels.

Can the networks REALLY afford to lose 15 million passionate, dedicated soap opera viewers every day? Of course not. Wake up, executives! Societal changes have affected ratings, with many women not home in the afternoon anymore and girls no longer automatically getting the soap habit from their moms. But millions of people watch TV now on DVR, TiVo, Hulu, ABC.com, etc. The housewife of yesterday is the busy working mom of today. She still likes to be entertained and have an escape from reality, but on her own time. She has all the same experiences and desires as the women who listened to soaps on the radio, except she shares them now on Facebook and Twitter instead of at the corner grocery.

The soaps that do remain on the air today continue to be very special. They must be cherished and protected like a beloved family member, or they could be lost.

How special are they? I'm glad you asked...

CUE OPENING COMMERCIAL...

CHAPTER 1
In The Beginning...

...was the word and the word was soap. Selling it, that is. And a highly unlikely person figured out how to do it.

It was the 1920s, and the country was skidding towards The Great Depression. Motion pictures were adding sound. Charles Lindbergh proved how "Lucky" he was by making the first transatlantic solo airplane flight. The sale of alcohol was illegal (yeah, right). Radio was gaining traction as the first mass broadcasting medium, bringing news and entertainment into people's living rooms. Consequently, radio advertising exploded, as ad agencies and sponsors looked for innovative ways to sell products to the home listener, many of whom were housewives. But how best to reach them?

In 1926, NBC Radio in Chicago launched a 15-minute program aimed at housewives. "The Women's Magazine of the Air" was designed to give helpful tips to women on how to keep a home more efficiently. Procter & Gamble was one of the original sponsors of this new "radio magazine," using the show to sell Camay and Ivory soap. Thus began a long association that would end over 80 years later, when P&G broke the hearts of millions of soap fans by walking away from the medium. But we're getting ahead of ourselves…

"The Women's Magazine of the Air" was a hit. Wow, who knew women could do housework and listen to the radio at the same time? Soon after "The Women's Magazine of the Air" debuted, a small, plain-looking, Jewish school teacher named Irna Phillips talked her way into a job at WGN Radio in Chicago. (The call letters stood for "World's Greatest Newspaper," *The Chicago Tribune*). Irna was a plain girl, who had already suffered through the death of her father at age 8, the subsequent struggles of her mother to raise ten children alone, and a reported stillborn baby as an unmarried 19 year-old. It was a sad start to her life, albeit excellent training for soap opera storytelling.

Desperate to become an actress, Irna Phillips was hired to do voice-overs and acting on various radio shows. She also showed an aptitude for writing, thanks to her teaching background. As one of the few women at the station, Phillips was soon asked to create a 15-minute radio show along the lines of "The Women's Magazine of the Air," but with the request that it be about a family. Phillips, who was still living with her mom, rolled up her single gal sleeves and created "Painted Dreams." The rest is soap opera history.

"Painted Dreams" debuted in 1930. It is considered the first radio serial, because Phillips recognized that she needed to keep her stories going to make listeners tune in every day, as well as market the show specifically for product tie-ins. According to The Museum of Television & Radio, Phillips said it must "actually sell merchandise; otherwise the object of radio advertising has failed." "Painted Dreams" was a success, but in the first of many soap opera moments of her career, Phillips lost the copyright to WGN after she insisted they take the show national, and was banned from having anything more to do with the program.

Having learned something from her heroines at this point, Phillips quickly created a similar show called "Today's Children" for the competition, WMAQ. The opening of "Today's Children" laid the groundwork for all future soap opera storytelling with this opening: "And today's children with their hopes and dreams, their laughter and tears, shall be the builders of a better world tomorrow."

"World" would turn out to be a very prescient word for Phillips.

AND A LITTLE LADY SHALL LEAD THEM

With "Today's Children" up and running (and selling soap to all those clever housewives able to listen and clean at the same time), Phillips got the idea for a "never-ending saga," based on a kindly minister named Dr. John Ruthledge and his troubled flock in a small town called Five Points. She called it "The Guiding Light."

"The Guiding Light" debuted on CBS Radio in 1937, sponsored by Procter & Gamble, which was now completely sold on the concept of the 15-minute radio serial. "There is a destiny that makes us brothers," read Reverend Ruthledge on the first episode (quoting poet Edwin Markham). "None goes his way alone. All that we send into the lives of others, comes back into our own."

And thus was the term "soap opera" coined: "Soap" for the sponsors, and "opera" for the heartfelt, throat-clutching drama. Phillips' talent for complex, timely storytelling shone immediately with tales of Minister Ruthledge's daughter Mary befriending a Jewish girl named Rose, one of the very first social issue stories on a radio soap. At the height of the war, Phillips scripted a World War II vet discussing his disability on a radio broadcast, listened to and discussed by the fictional people in Five Points. John Ruthledge frequently gave sermons about how faith and patience would lead to happiness, which became so popular with listeners they were collected into a book that sold almost 300,000 copies. The title of "The Guiding Light" referred to a lamp Ruthledge kept in his window to "guide" his flock. His sermons (okay,

Irna's) did the same.

Soon after "The Guiding Light" hit the airwaves, Phillips' beloved mother passed away. Since she had based the matriarch of "Today's Children" on her mom, naming the character Mother Moran and voicing the character herself, Phillips insisted NBC cancel the show in deference to her mother's memory. NBC agreed. (Can you imagine?)

Phillips replaced "Today's Children" with "Woman in White," the first serial drama set in a hospital, where she hired young future legend Agnes Nixon. Phillips followed that with "The Road of Life" in 1938 and "The Right to Happiness" in 1939.

By 1943, the prolific Irna Phillips had five 15-minute radio soap operas on the air. Rather than write the dialogue into a standard script, Phillips would act the stories out, playing every part while a secretary wrote down the dialogue. She was an aspiring actress, after all. Eventually, she hired assistants to fill in some of the dialogue that she couldn't act out herself.

At times, Phillips would be rewriting the script until minutes before the show went on the air live, forcing some poor assistant to race down the hall flinging pages to the actors as the director counted down "5-4-3-2..." It was during this time that Phillips pioneered many of the devices now commonly associated with soap operas. She was the first to use organ music (dun-dun-*DUN*) between scenes, and when cutting to commercials. She was the first to "cliff-hang" the listener to make them tune in tomorrow. She was the first to hire a real doctor and lawyer to advise her on the accuracy of her scripts, because she was also the first to recognize the importance of the hospital and the courtroom to soap opera storytelling.

Recognizing that homemakers had to do chores while listening to her shows, Phillips was careful to keep the pace of her shows slow and steady so the busy housewife didn't miss anything. Hence, the soap staple of recapping ("Could you believe it yesterday when so-and-so did *this?*") was also perfected by Phillips.

"You have to remember that there are always shades of gray with people," explained Phillips. "Nobody is all good or all bad and each human being can exhibit all of these different elements, often at the same time."

At the height of her radio career, Phillips was responsible for 2 million words a year. As a result, she earned $250,000 a year, which was unheard of for anyone at that time, much less a woman.

It's pretty good by today's standards, too.

EVERYBODY INTO THE POOL!

Naturally, with the success of Irna Phillips' soap operas on radio, other players got into the game. Frank and Anne Hummert were a husband-and-wife team from an ad agency who started writing shows in the 1930s. They felt housewives needed more of a fantasy escape from their humdrum lives, so they created stories with a lot more romance and fantasy than Phillips' realistic fare provided. Think: Romance novel on radio.

The Hummerts radio efforts included "Backstage Wife," which paired a girl from small town Iowa with a rich, famous Broadway star, and "Our Gal Sunday" which united a miner's daughter with a fancy titled Englishman. The duo quickly had 12 radio soaps on the air, necessitating a writing team for each show that set the stage for the way soaps

time. Stu's portrayer, Larry Haines, won three Emmys in the role. Stuart played heroine Jo from the show's first episode in 1951 to its last episode in 1986, a daytime television feat met only by the legendary Susan Lucci.

"It was a marvelous time," the late Stuart told the Museum of Television and Radio of those early days. "We had to create reality out of almost nothing. The stories moved so slowly that to fill the time [and] make the relationships real required so much from the actors. It was all in the listening, the faces." As Stuart outlines, there was a steep learning curve for the former radio writers to successfully transition their storylines to television. It wasn't enough to just write "doorbell rings" in a script, like it was when the soaps were on radio. Whose door was it? Where was the bell? What was happening on the doorstep? What was the weather like? Who was inside the house?

Stuart recalled an exec who went ballistic when there was no such direction in an early script. "The script said 'This scene takes place at the mailbox'," remembered Stuart. "He said, 'What is behind the mailbox? Where is the mailbox? You can't just say the mailbox.' It's so obvious now, but in the early days the writers were just learning."

Soap writers had an advantage over other kinds of writers, though, because they were accustomed to using dialogue *alone* to tell their stories on radio. That created a connection with their devoted audience that continues to this day. Winsor recognized this, and consequently used bare kitchen and living room sets on "Search For Tomorrow," knowing that the relationship between his characters and his viewers would sell his show. Nobody cared what kind of couch Jo was sitting on when she poured her heart out to Stu and the other good folks in Henderson, USA. The camera just zoomed in on her troubled, expressive face, and the viewer was hooked.

"She was box office from day one," bragged Winsor.

IRNA'S "WORLD"

Ten months after "Search for Tomorrow" debuted, Irna Phillips successfully transitioned "The Guiding Light" from radio to television. It was produced by Procter & Gamble Productions, as would be all of Irna Phillips' future TV soaps. Although it was an immediate TV hit, "The

Guiding Light" also remained on the radio for the next four years. This set up an exhausting schedule for the actors, since both were live. Now broadcasting from New York City (where the radio show had moved in 1949), the cast had to run down the street from the CBS television studio to the radio station, where they repeated the same program later that same day. That was crazier than some of the stories they were telling.

In the 15 years since "The Guiding Light" had debuted on radio, the focus had shifted from Reverend Ruthledge's flock in Five Points to the Bauer family in Springfield, led by wise matriarch Bert. Actress Charita Bauer (funny coincidence, huh?) had started playing Bert Bauer on radio in 1950, and was one of the few actors to successfully make the transition to TV. Bert evolved into the heart of the show, standing by her alcoholic husband Bill and becoming the "guiding light" for her large family.

During this time, Phillips brought Agnes Nixon on board as a co-head writer. Nixon proved herself a worthy graduate of the Irna Phillips School of Social Issues by giving Bert Bauer uterine cancer, which educated millions of viewers on the importance of Pap Smears. The Bauers remained an

important family in Springfield until "Guiding Light" went
off the air in 2009. *(Note: "The" was dropped from the title in
1975.)*

Early stories on TV included way too much drinking,
unwanted pregnancies, and wanton women, set against the
backdrop of an ad agency. Sound familiar, "Mad Men" fans?
Some of these stories were written by a young Chicagoan
named William J. Bell, hired in 1956, another Phillips protégé who would go on to become a soap legend.   "Guiding
Light" holds the record for the longest-running scripted series
in television history (57 years; 1952-2009), and is second
only to "Meet the Press" in longevity of all TV shows.

Not content to have one hit soap on the air, Phillips
set about creating the first half-hour soap in 1956: "As The
World Turns." Recognizing the enormous challenge, Phillips lured Agnes Nixon back from "Search For Tomorrow" to
co-write the show, and hired another future soap legend Ted
Corday to direct and produce. "As The World Turns" would
be Irna Phillips' crowning glory.

"Good morning, dear," said homemaker Nancy
Hughes to her husband Chris, opening a historic 54-year long

run on television. The longer format gave Phillips the chance to explore relationships within more than one main family, making the "haves" and "have-nots" a running theme. Scenes were longer. Characters had dramatic conversations over coffee as the camera lingered on their faces. Pregnant pauses as the organ music swelled became another soap staple.

Billed as the "day-to-day story of the affections that bind - and the conflicts that threaten - two closely related families in an American community," the show pitted the Hughes family against the Lowells in good, ole Oakdale, IL. Chris Hughes's sister Edith quickly took center stage, which was not surprising since she was played by former film star Ruth Warrick (*Citizen Kane*; Warrick later went on to soap stardom as "All My Children's" Phoebe Tyler). Edith had a torrid affair with Jim Lowell, and encouraged her impressionable young niece Penny to become more "liberated" by getting involved with dreamy Jeff Baker. Penny and Jeff became soaps' first teen storyline, creating what Schemering called "soap opera's first stars" in actors Rosemary Prinz and Mark Rydell. Penny and Jeff suffered alcoholism (his), miscarriage (hers) and annulment (theirs) on the road to their inevitable split.

In 1962, Rydell broke the news to Irna Phillips that he wanted to become a director. Knowing fans would never buy another actor in the role, she decided to kill Jeff in a car wreck. Fans went berserk, flooding CBS with complaint calls, letters and telegrams. TV Guide called it the "automobile accident that shook the nation."

It worked out pretty well for Rydell, though. He went on to direct 1981 Best Picture nominee *On Golden Pond*.

Meanwhile, in a shocking shift from all previous soap storytelling, Phillips decided to set the action around a scheming vixen instead of a heroine like Jo Tate or Bert Bauer, so she created Lisa Miller, played by Eileen Fulton. Lisa used every trick in the book to catch men, and she didn't care that most of them already belonged to other women. She soon set her sights on nice guy Bob Hughes, played by Don Hastings, despite disapproval from his parents and most of their neighbors. Lisa even had the nerve to *hire someone else to clean her house*, while she went out. In one hilarious scene, Nancy Hughes complimented Lisa on what a clean house she kept, and Lisa simply said "Thank you."

That outraged 1960s housewives even more than her affairs.

"They hated her," Fulton told NPR, "and I thought it was fabulous. I'd only been on the show a few weeks, and I was standing in front of Lord & Taylor. This beautifully dressed woman in a Chanel suit – in the days before there were knockoffs – came up to me and said, 'Aren't you Lisa?' And I said, 'Yes, that's the part I play.' And she said, 'I hate you,' and she hit me. Then a telegram came into the studio. It said, 'If that bitch Lisa marries Bob, I'll never watch "As the World Turns" again.' That is how the character was truly locked in."

"As The World Turns" quickly overtook "The Guiding Light" and "Search For Tomorrow." It became the number one soap in 1959 and stayed at the top of the ratings for a stunning 12 years. By the mid-1960s, a full 50% of the day-time audience was watching Lisa's naughty exploits. In fact, Lisa was so popular, Phillips spun her off onto her own prime-time show called "Our Private World," which she co-created with William J. Bell. The spin-off aired on Wednesdays and

Fridays over the summer of 1965, but was short-lived. Irna Phillips had spread her favorite bad girl a little too thin.

Or perhaps Phillips was just too busy. In 1964, she pioneered the hour-long soap with NBC's "Another World," also co-created with Bell. One of their first stories involved the forbidden subject of abortion. When teenager Pat Matthews became pregnant, she had an illegal abortion that left her sterile. Naturally, she hunted down the boyfriend that got her pregnant and shot him. "Another World" was also the first soap to do a crossover, when Mike Bauer traveled from "The Guiding Light's" Springfield to "Another World's" Bay City. Although both shows were created by Phillips and produced by P&G, they aired on different networks, so that was quite a feat. Phillips followed that with "Days of Our Lives" in 1965, co-created with her former director Ted Corday and his wife, Betty. (Their son Ken Corday still runs the show today on NBC.)

"Love Is A Many Splendored Thing" followed in 1967, the first soap based on a movie; the 1955 film of the same name. Here, Phillips pioneered the first interracial love story with Eurasian Mia and American Viet Nam war pilot

Paul Bradley. CBS exec Fred Silverman proclaimed the story too controversial and ordered Phillips to kill it. She refused, and quit. Not surprisingly, "Love Is A Many Splendored Thing" only ran six years. But it did launch the careers of future soap uber-producer John Conboy, and actresses Leslie Charleson (Monica Quartermaine, "General Hospital") and Donna Mills (troublemaker Abby on "Knots Landing"). *Note: All of these shows aired live when they debuted. One by one, they went from live to pre-recorded on tape, and from black and white to color, except for "Days," which debuted in color. The 15-minute shows eventually went to a half hour, then the half hour shows to an hour. "Another World" actually went to 90 minutes in 1979-80, but soon reverted back to an hour.*

LIGHTS OUT

As the years went on, Phillips set more and more of her drama in hospitals, illustrating her hypochondria and fascination with her own "ailments." "None of us is a stranger to success and failure, life and death, the need to be loved, the struggle to communicate with another human being, a corroding sense of loneliness," said Phillips to *McCall's* magazine in 1965. "My life is completely different from the average woman's, but because we share the same essential hopes and fears, what is true of her is true of me."

It's sad to think that the woman who created love in the afternoon may never have experienced it herself. But while she never married, she did adopt a boy and a girl when she was in her 40s.

Although all of her shows were eventually based in New York, Phillips never left Chicago. She flew in or did business by phone. Deeply engrossed in her stories and characters, she kept careful track of them all, and always called her actors by their character's names.

She was also famously difficult; P&G execs were said to be scared to death of her. Schemering tells the story of the time Eileen Fulton accidentally dropped one of her "As The World Turns" scripts. A petrified P&G employee picked it up, admonishing Fulton that "An Irna Phillips script is like the flag. It never touches the floor."

Never one to pay much attention to the real world, Irna saw Barry Goldwater on TV in 1964 and asked who he was. After being informed that he was the Republican presidential candidate, she pronounced: "Good casting."

By the 1970s, Phillips' method of character-based, family-oriented storytelling had grown tame against the backdrop of Viet Nam protests and "Burn Your Bra" marches. The students became the teachers, as Agnes Nixon debuted the social-issue based "One Life To Live" on ABC in 1968 and "All My Children" in 1970, while William J. Bell brought the sexually charged "The Young and the Restless" to CBS in 1973.

After 12 years at number one, "As The World Turns" was finally overtaken in the ratings by "General Hospital" and Phillips' own "Days of our Lives" in the early 1970s.

In a bid to turn things around, Phillips concocted a plot where Bob Hughes, who had divorced Lisa and married Jennifer, went to a medical conference and slept with Jennifer's sister, a liberated widow named Kim. Bob made plans to leave Jennifer until she announced that she was pregnant with his child. Kim also turned up pregnant, so she married Bob's rival, Dr. John Dixon, to keep the paternity secret. (Trivia: That baby was Sabrina Hughes, played 14 years later by a young Julianne Moore.) While that sounds like a pretty tame soap story by today's standards, fans were revolted by kindly

Dr. Bob sleeping with his sister-in-law.

"When Kim seduced Bob, the audience was very

shocked," admitted Bob's portrayer, Don Hastings, to the

Museum of Broadcasting. "She and her sister were both preg-

nant [by Bob]. Some people didn't like that, but others stood

by him. If the writers had Bob kill someone there are a lot

of people out there who would make excuses for him. They

would say, 'Oh, well, the gun went off.'"

But despite some viewers' fierce loyalty to Bob, ratings

fell further.

And then the axe fell.

Irna Phillips' harshest soap opera moment came in

1973, when she was cruelly fired by P&G, despite having

created their entire stable of soap operas and selling billions

of dollars' worth of their detergent, toothpaste, diapers and

yes, soap. Unable to take inspiration from any of her own

heroines - or a rousing Reverend Ruthledge sermon - Phillips

died heartbroken later that year. Fortunately for soap fans,

she left her proteges Agnes Nixon and William J. Bell behind

to lead a raucous renaissance in the 1970s and 80s - and keep the lamp lit in the window.

CHAPTER 2
Shining a Light on Soaps

I rna Phillips created a soap opera juggernaut of passion and devotion that continues to this day. Of the six television soap operas currently airing now, five of them have direct ties to Irna:

* Irna co-created "Days of our Lives" with Ted and Betty Corday.

* Her protégé Agnes Nixon created "All My Children" and "One Life To Live."

* Her protege William J. Bell created "The Young and the Restless" and "The Bold and the Beautiful" with his wife, Lee Phillip Bell.

Only "General Hospital" didn't come out of the Phillips mill - it was created by Frank and Doris Hursley, who had written for "Search for Tomorrow."

Nixon and Bell were trained by the best, and their shows reflected it every day on ABC and CBS. But unlike Phillips, their roads to success were far less dramatic.

RECAP: AGNES NIXON

Agnes Nixon began her career as a dialogue writer on Phillips' radio soap "Woman in White," where she learned about the forbidden love between (married) doctors and nurses. She went on to work at "Search For Tomorrow" before joining "The Guiding Light" and working her way up to the position of Head Writer.

After showing fans the "Light," Nixon moved on to Phillips' other babies "As The World Turns" and "Another World," all the while working on her own creations that would showcase diversity. She felt strongly that soaps should have black characters and families, and not all be set in "Whiteville."

"One Life To Live" debuted on ABC in 1968, set in the fictional blue-collar town of Llanview, PA. Troubled heroine Victoria Lord was the heart of the show, and remains so to this day, still played 40 years later by six-time Emmy winner Erika Slezak.

Nixon proved she meant interracial business by crafting the story of a light-skinned black nurse named Carla Gray, who was passing for white. (Get it? She wasn't black or white, she was *GRAY*.) The audience knew of her ruse because they watched her apply her "white" makeup, but the white doctor and black intern courting Carla did not. Talk about a complicated love triangle.

Two years later, Nixon debuted "All My Children," also on ABC. Here, Nixon took a page from "As The World Turns's" bitchy Lisa Miller and built her new show around a similar character: teenage vixen Erica Kane, played by Susan Lucci (duh). Lucci remains "All My Children's" only original contract actor, and is still front and center 40 years later.

And yes, she did finally win that Best Actress Emmy after 19 nominations in 1999.

In real life, Agnes Eckhardt Nixon enjoyed a long marriage to Robert Nixon after suffering through the death of her college sweetheart in a plane crash. They had four children.   Once, when Nixon was in labor, she brought a tape recorder to the hospital so she could continue working while she delivered the baby. Apparently, her motto "Make 'em laugh, make 'em cry, make 'em wait" applied to all HER children, too.

Widowed since 1996, Nixon lives in Pennsylvania, where both her shows are set. She continues to consult at ABC at age 83.

RECAP: WILLIAM J. BELL

Phillips' other progeny, William J. Bell, got his start as a dialogue writer on "The Guiding Light." He co-wrote "As The World Turns" with Irna Phillips for nine years before moving to "Days of our Lives" as Head Writer. While there, Bell experimented with stories of forbidden love - like disfigured, amnesiac soldier Tommy Horton who returned from the war and fell in love with his own sister, Marie - which later became a staple on his own soaps, "The Young and the Restless" and "The Bold and the Beautiful."

Bell left "Days" to create "The Young and the Restless" in 1972, but "Days" sued him for leaving. He ended up staying on as head writer of "Days" until 1975, creating the bizarre situation where he was the head writer of two soap operas competing against each other for two full years.

"The Young and the Restless" started out last in the ratings, but slowly inched its way up to overtake "Days" during the 1975 season. By the time Bell left "Days" to work full-time on his own creation, "The Young and the Restless" was third in the ratings (after "As The World Turns" and "Another World"). "Days" had dropped to fifth.

"The Bold and the Beautiful" debuted on March 23, 1987 and remains the only half-hour soap. Cleverly marketed internationally with beautiful people and universal themes, it eventually spread to over 100 countries and is the most-watched soap opera in the world. Adding to its international appeal, characters have sex on practically every episode. When Taylor yells out Ridge's name while she's in bed with Whip, it is deliciously awkward in every language.

Bill and Lee Bell had three children, all of whom work in the family business. Oldest son William J. Bell, Jr., is the president of Bell Dramatic Serial Company and Bell-Phillip Television Productions, Inc., the companies that oversee both shows. His wife Maria Arena Bell, who interned as a writer under Bill Sr. at "The Bold and the Beautiful" before marrying his son, is Executive Producer and Head Writer of "The Young and the Restless."

Bradley Bell is Executive Producer and Head Writer of "The Bold and the Beautiful." His wife Colleen Bell is an LA-based philanthropist. Lauralee Bell is an actress, who got her start as Christine "Cricket" Blair on "The Young and the Restless" at age 15 and has played the role sporadically ever since. She is wed to photographer Scott Martin.

William J. Bell died in 2005 of complications related to Alzheimer's. His children are carrying on his legacy in the same way he carried on Irna Phillips'.

THE EDGE OF RIGHT

The shows created by Agnes Nixon and Bill Bell exploded in the go-go 1970's and 80's.

In January, 1973, the landmark case of Jane Roe v. Dallas District Attorney Henry Wade was decided by the Supreme Court in favor of Roe, granting women the right to obtain a legal abortion in all 50 states.

Agnes Nixon, Queen of the Social Issue Story, jumped right on that, scripting television's first legal abortion for "All My Children" vixen Erica Kane that very same year. In the story, Erica found herself pregnant by her husband Jeff Martin, a big problem for a girl dreaming of a modeling career. Erica secretly aborted the baby, which ironically didn't do as much damage to her marriage as her affair with her agent, Jason Maxwell.

Surprisingly, there was little backlash to Erica's abortion. The country was, for the most part, behind the legislation and changing at a rapid rate, so a character like Erica legally ending a pregnancy didn't stir much controversy. It probably helped that Erica was the bad girl of the show, and would have made a terrible mother at that time.

Nixon also hedged her bets by scripting a post-abortion infection called toxoplasmosis for Erica, insuring that she would be punished. The ABC switchboards lit up with well wishes from fans - as well as calls from doctors and nurses on how to treat their favorite vixen.

Nixon also broke new ground when Martin family matriarch Ruth Martin protested the Vietnam War after her son Phil was drafted. A soap character speaking out against a real war was unheard of, but once again Nixon had taken the temperature of the nation and responded accordingly through her stories. Fans responded positively, and Ruth's portrayer Mary Fickett won the very first Daytime Lead Actress Emmy.

"I didn't feel that took so much courage," said Nixon in 1987. "It was like a mother speaking."

Prostitution, drug addiction, AIDS, interracial romance and domestic violence are just some of the other pressing issues Nixon has addressed on both "All My Children" and sister show "One Life To Live." She also told the first story of father/daughter incest on "Loving," a half-hour soap she created with Doug Marland in 1983. ("Loving" morphed into "The City" in 1995 and was canceled in 1997. It was replaced by "General Hospital" spinoff "Port Charles.")

In true Irna Phillips style, all of these problems are always told through the eyes of a family, and how they impact the people they love. William J. Bell also addressed social issues, but it was the way he addressed sexual freedom that put his shows on the map. No twin beds for Bell's characters on "The Young and the Restless!"

The rich Brooks and Chancellor families and the middle class Fosters dealt head-on with premarital sex, birth control, infidelity and impotence. Even a couple in the throes of a divorce, like Phillip and Katherine Chancellor, played their scenes on a set packed with fresh flowers and crystal decanters full of the booze that was killing her. "Yes, I will sign your damnable papers!" cried Katherine as she gulped vodka from a crystal glass and then sunk to the expensive Oriental rug, weeping.

Bell put together the prettiest cast on daytime, gave them lush sets full of fresh flowers and soft lighting, and then had them slowly disrobe as sensual music played. It was just as common to see Chris and Snapper Foster in bed as it was to see young Paul Williams and Lauren Fenmore in the shower.

Bell didn't start the sexual revolution, but he sure moved it along.

WHERE THE ART IS

"The Young and the Restless" has been the #1 soap for 22 years in a row. Here's where some of the most successful modern soap operas stack up, along with a few tidbits about them. The current shows are listed in chronological order, followed by the three big P&G shows no longer airing.

GENERAL HOSPITAL

DEBUT: ABC on April 1, 1963. Went to 45 minutes in 1976 and an hour in 1978.

CREATORS: Frank and Doris Hursley

SET IN: Port Charles, NY

NOTED FOR: Fantastic, long-running characters. Steve and Audrey Hardy, Jessie Brewer, Luke and Laura Spencer, the Quartermaines, Robert, Anna and Robin Scorpio, Sonny

Corinthos, and Jason Morgan (formerly Quartermaine) to name just a few.

"GH" also boasts the greatest turnaround in soap history. On the verge of being canceled in 1977, ABC hired former "Search for Tomorrow" director Gloria Monty as Executive Producer, and Doug Marland (who had worked for Irna Phillips at "As The World Turns" and "Another World") as Head Writer, to turn the show around. Marland scripted the tortured teen triangle of Laura/Scotty/Bobbie and Rick and Monica's affair behind Lesley and Alan's backs, while Monty sped up the action and improved production values. "GH" shot up - and then along came Luke.

MEMORABLE STORY: Mikkos Cassadine threatened to blackmail the world with his ability to freeze temperatures by producing carbonic snow. The formula was located in the base of the Ice Princess, which was the world's largest uncut diamond (painted black to conceal it). Luke, Laura and Robert foiled the plan by uncovering the code to Mikkos's dastardly machine (password: ICE PRINCESS) and freezing him to death instead.

MY FAVORITE SCENE: Anna tying up her ex-husband Robert on Valentines Day, 1991, after he insulted her. "Do you think I look like an old hag?" she taunted as she pranced around him in her lingerie. "I am sexy. I know how to turn someone on. I know how to get dressed up. And I know how to tie someone up, obviously."

DAYS OF OUR LIVES

DEBUT: NBC on November 8, 1965. Went to an hour in 1975.

CREATORS: Irna Phillips, Ted and Betty Corday. Show is still co-owned by Corday Productions, run by their son Ken Corday.

SET IN: Salem, USA

NOTED FOR: "Like sands through the hour glass, so are the days of our lives." That opening is still read at the top of each episode by former star Macdonald Carey (Tom Horton), despite the fact that he died in 1994. Members of the Horton family remain front and center, most notably Hope, Maggie and Jennifer. "Days" has always told the most outrageous stories, which is saying something for soaps. The toppers were Vivian burying Carly alive, Stefano planting a chip in Hope's brain to turn her into Evil Gina, and "killing" the cast and then having them turn up on a faraway island called Melaswen, which was "New Salem" spelled backwards. But the biggest was...

MEMORABLE STORY: Dr. Marlena Evans was possessed by the devil in 1994 and 95. Her eyes turned yellow and she actually levitated up off the bed. While possessed, Marlena chloroformed Kristen, chained her to the church altar and set the church on fire, caused a heat wave, caused animals to attack, and lit the Salem town Christmas tree on fire. Fortunately, Marlena's former lover (and future husband) John Black thought he was a priest, so he exorcised her.

MY FAVORITE STORY: John and Marlena committing adultery in 1993 on the conference room desk at Titan Publishing (which conceived Belle)... and Sami catching them.

ONE LIFE TO LIVE

DEBUT: ABC on July 15, 1968. Went to 45 minutes in
1976 and an hour in 1978.

CREATOR: Agnes Nixon

SET IN: Llanview, PA

NOTED FOR: Victoria Lord has been the show's heroine
since its inception. Viki was originally played by Gillian
Spencer, who had played Peggy on "Guiding Light" and went
on to play Daisy Cortlandt on "All My Children" in an Agnes
Nixon trifecta. Erika Slezak took over in 1971 and has played
Viki ever since. Viki has DID (Disassociative Identity Disorder) which causes multiple personalities. This has garnered
Slezak six Daytime Emmys for playing Viki, Niki, Jean, et
al, the most Emmys of any actress. Viki vs. Dorian Lord, her
former stepmother, is daytime's longest female rivalry. The
Buchanan family was introduced in 1979, based on JR Ew-
ing and his family on the prime-time hit "Dallas." Robert S.
Woods still plays Bo Buchanan over 30 years later.

MEMORABLE STORY: In 1979, Dr. Larry Wolek's wife Karen was called to testify in Marco Dane's murder trial. Herb Callison relentlessly cross-examined Karen until she admitted Marco was blackmailing her. "Oh God, I can't watch this," murmured knowing defendant Viki, as she covered her eyes. Herb read a list of men and then forced the nice housewife to admit she was actually a prostitute. "I was a common hooker and Marco Dane was my pimp," sobbed Karen. "Is that what you want from me? You want me to say I am scum? Talbot Huddleston was my first john, the first of so many men I don't even remember their names! There - are you SATISFIED?"

By the end of this long, riveting scene, Karen had had a complete breakdown on the witness stand. Her portrayer, Judith Light, won back-to-back Lead Actress Emmys in 1980 and '81, before leaving the soap to star in "Who's the Boss?" and "Ugly Betty."

MY FAVORITE STORY: When Megan was dying of complications from Lupus on Valentine's Day 1992, Reverend Andrew Carpenter brought her true love Jake back to Llanview to be with her. Jake carried Megan to the window so she could see their special tree, which he had covered in red hearts. As one of those red hearts slipped slowly out of her hand, Megan died in Jake's arms.

ALL MY CHILDREN

DEBUT: ABC on January 5, 1970 as a half-hour show. Went to an hour in 1977. Virtually none of the half-hour episodes exist today - ABC taped over them.

CREATOR: Agnes Nixon. The title of the show refers to the "bonds of humanity," and the photo album in the opening credits features a poem written by Nixon:

> *The Great and the Least,*
> *The Rich and the Poor,*
> *The Weak and the Strong,*
> *In Sickness and in Health,*
> *In Joy and Sorrow,*
> *In Tragedy and Triumph,*
> *You are ALL MY CHILDREN*

SET IN: Pine Valley, PA

NOTED FOR: Daytime's longest running original character

Erica Kane, played by Susan Lucci of course. Social issue stories, and sweet romances like Cliff and Nina, Greg and Jenny, Angie and Jesse, Tad and Dixie. The famous rivalry between Palmer Cortlandt and Adam Chandler, whose humble roots had both been in Pigeon Hollow, TN.

Interestingly, Nixon brought on former "As The World Turns" star Rosemary Prinz (Penny) as a "special guest star" for the show's first six months to play Amy Tyler. Nixon had worked with soap and stage actress Prinz on "World Turns," and wanted to draw that soap's fans to her new show. It worked.

MEMORABLE STORY: Scheming Liza Colby plotted to get Greg back after he left her for Tad's sister, Jenny. When Jesse Hubbard pushed Liza during an argument while defending Jenny, Liza tore her own clothes and claimed rape. Jesse ran away to New York where he saved Jenny from a porno career; the charges were dropped. Meanwhile, back in Pine Valley, Tad the Cad earned his nickname by taking Liza's virginity and then bedding her mother, Marian Colby.

MY FAVORITE SCENE: Erica faces down a bear in the woods in 1985. "Get away from me, you disgusting beast. You may not come near me, do you understand? I am Erica Kane - and YOU are a filthy beast!"

THE YOUNG AND THE RESTLESS

DEBUT: CBS on March 26, 1973 as a half-hour show. Went to an hour in 1980.

CREATORS: William J. and Lee Phillip Bell

SET IN: Genoa City, WI

NOTED FOR: Nikki and Victor Newman have been daytime's most popular and star-crossed couple since the early 1980s. Victor Newman and Jack Abbott enjoy daytime's longest male rivalry.

In 1991-92, Bell pulled off one of daytime's most shocking storylines, when he killed Sheila Carter (who had kidnapped Lauren's baby at birth and swapped it for another) in a fire on "The Young and the Restless," and then had her turn up months later as a nurse at Forrester Creations on sister show "The Bold and the Beautiful."

MEMORABLE STORY: David Kimball was a murderer trying to escape the law, so he hired a plastic surgeon to make him look like David Hasselhoff. (Inside joke: Hasselhoff had gotten his start playing Snapper Foster on the show.) Instead, the surgeon carved the word KILLER on David's forehead. David covered his forehead in makeup and donned a disguise, but was found out by Detective Paul Williams. To escape, David hid in a garbage chute. He was subsequently crushed to death by the trash compactor.

MY FAVORITE SCENE: When Victor ousted his hated rival Jack from Jack's family company, Jabot, he demanded Jack vacate the CEO's office. "I want you out of that chair," ordered Victor.

"You want this chair?" retorted Jack, throwing it out the high-rise window and shattering glass everywhere. "Have a seat."

THE BOLD AND THE BEAUTIFUL

DEBUT: CBS on March 23, 1987 as a half-hour show. Remains daytime's only half-hour soap.

CREATOR: William J. and Lee Phillip Bell

SET IN: Los Angeles, CA

NOTED FOR: It is the only show set in a real place, and the only one simulcast in Spanish using SAP. It is set in a fashion house called Forrester Creations, founded by Eric and run by his son Ridge. Ridge and Brooke are also one of daytime's longest running couples. "B&B" boasts four actors from its first year, the most of any soap. They are John McCook (Eric), Susan Flannery (Stephanie), Ronn Moss (Ridge) and Katherine Kelly Lang (Brooke).

MEMORABLE STORY: In 1994, Taylor Forrester was presumed dead in a plane crash in the Middle East. A grieving Ridge turned to Brooke. Taylor turned up with amnesia in Morocco being cared for by Prince Omar who called her

"Princess Laila." When Taylor's memory returned, she elected to stay in Morocco because she saw how happy Ridge and Brooke were. She eventually returned to LA when her father had a heart attack, and was discovered to be alive. She's been after Ridge ever since.

MY FAVORITE STORY: In 1993, Eric Forrester planned to wed evil baby-napper Sheila Carter. Lauren shredded Sheila's wedding dress the night before the nuptials, but that didn't stop the determined bride. Eric's family, however, did - by showing up to the ceremony dressed in funereal black. Sheila ran out, declaring she couldn't get married without the support of Eric's family. Eric and Sheila then wed privately, but the marriage was short-lived.

GUIDING LIGHT

DEBUT: Radio in 1937, and CBS television in 1952.

CREATOR: Irna Phillips

SET IN: Springfield, USA

NOTED FOR: In addition to everything covered in the previous chapter, Reva Shayne!

MEMORABLE STORY: Reva, played so memorably by multiple Emmy winner Kim Zimmer, went through Lewis men like a tsunami on a quiet beach. Her marriage to true love Josh's father, HB, made Josh so mad he crashed his car and was paralyzed. Josh later confronted her in one of daytime's most memorable scenes ever.

> *Josh (outside at a party): "Well, well, well. The cripple and the tramp have cleared the place out."*
> *Reva: "You want me to be a slut? I'll be a slut. Old Reva ain't nothing if she ain't obliging. (Strips down to her skivvies.) Here she is, folks: Reva Shayne Lewis. Tramp. Adulteress. Scarlet woman. (Jumps into the fountain.) I baptize myself the Slut of Springfield! Is that what you want? Call everybody out here. The more the merrier! You look at me like I'm naked, like I don't have a heart or a brain. All your dirty mind sees is my body. Well, here it is. You take a good look."*

MY FAVORITE STORY: When Zimmer quit the show in 1990, "GL" scripted a fantastic exit where she became post-partum after the birth of son Shayne and drove her car off a bridge in the Florida Keys. "I'm coming, Bud!" she yelled to Josh as he stood on the beach and screamed, "NOOOOOO!" Zimmer headed to Hollywood (where she memorably played Mr. Pitt's assistant on "Seinfeld" and starred on "Santa Barbara"), but was lured back to "GL" in 1995. The show wrote Reva back in as an Amish woman calling herself Rebecca suffering from amnesia in Goshen, Indiana. Alan Spaulding found her when she hit him with her carriage (!) and eventually brought her back to Springfield.

THE END: "GL" last aired on September 18, 2009 (see chapter 12 for more) and was replaced with "Let's Make A Deal." The last episode featured Josh returning to Springfield to see if Reva would keep the date they had made one year before to meet at The Lighthouse. She did, and they set off on a new adventure hand in hand.

AS THE WORLD TURNS

AIRED ON: CBS from April 2, 1956 to September 17, 2010.

CREATOR: Irna Phillips

SET IN: Oakdale, USA

NOTED FOR: In addition to everything covered in the previous chapter, the Snyder and Walsh families created by Doug Marland in the 80s.

MEMORABLE STORY: Teenaged heiress Lily Walsh came to town in 1984, and fell for hunky stable boy Holden Snyder, to the chagrin of her rich, snooty mother Lucinda Walsh. Lily grew very close to Holden's folksy mom Emma (modeled after Marland's own mother), and Holden's older sister, Iva. One day, Iva caught young Lily goofing around in the Snyder Pond with the much older Rod Landry and she flipped out. Turned out "Rod" was really Iva's cousin Josh Snyder who had raped Iva at 13 – and Lily was their biological daughter!

MY FAVORITE STORY: Handsome Scotsman Duncan McKechnie wed Shannon O'Hara in a beautiful ceremony at a Scottish castle, kilts and all, in the late 1980s. They were happy until his first wife, Lilith, came back and jealously went after poor Shannon, eventually killing her. Lilith sent proof of the murder to Duncan in the form of a shrunken head, which he accepted as confirmation that Shannon was dead. Naturally, she wasn't. Shannon returned years later with amnesia – after Duncan had wed Jessica.

THE END: "ATWT" was canceled for a talk show called "The Talk," starring Julie Chen, the wife of CBS honcho Les Moonves.

The last episode was a bit of a mess, because "ATWT" had replaced the much-loved actress Martha Byrne as Lily, so they couldn't end the show properly with Lily and Holden. (They did, however, awkwardly script the recast Lily "reminiscing" to Holden about meeting him as a stable boy. THUD.) Instead, Jack and Carly got remarried and Bob Hughes retired from the hospital.

Bob: *"Out of loss comes something great."*

Kim: *"I don't think there should be goodbyes. Just good-nights."*

Bob: *"Goodnight."*

And then Bob turned off the light and the WORLD stopped turning.

ANOTHER WORLD

AIRED ON: NBC on from May 4, 1964 to June 25, 1999. It was 30 minutes long from 1964-1975, and 60 minutes from 1975-1979. In 1979, Executive Producer Paul Rauch convinced NBC to extend the show to an unprecedented 90 minutes. Ratings were stagnant, so "AW" went back to one hour in 1980, spinning Mac Cory's daughter Iris Carrington (Beverlee McKinsey) onto her own show, "Texas," which ran through 1982.

CREATORS: Irna Phillips with William J. Bell

SET IN: Bay City, USA

NOTED FOR: "AW" was the first soap to address abortion, when teenager Pat Matthews illegally terminated her pregnancy in the show's first year. It also showcased the first and only theme song that made it to the Billboard Hot 100: "(You Take Me Away To) Another World" by Crystal Gayle and Gary Morris in 1987. Famed actress Robin Strasser (Dorian, "OLTL") got her start on "AW" as Rachel Cory in 1967. She was later replaced by Victoria Wyndham. Torrid couple Steve Frame (George Reinholt) and Alice Matthews (Jacqueline Courtney) heated up "AW" in the 1970s, but were let go amidst accusations of being difficult in 1975. They immediately jumped to rival "OLTL" as Tony Lord and Pat Ashley. All was eventually forgiven, and they both returned for big anniversary shows.

MEMORABLE STORIES: Mac's romance with the much younger Rachel inflamed his daughter Iris, and caused conflict for years. As a sign of their popularity, "AW" built its 25th anniversary episode in 1989 around Mac and Rachel, and the 25th anniversary of their magazine, Brava. Shortly before filming, Douglass Watson, who played Mac, died unexpectedly while on vacation. The Cory family hosted the celebration without Mac, welcoming back lots of former characters, including Steve and Alice. Watson's death was dealt with later that year when it was explained Mac had died offscreen.

MY FAVORITE STORY: When Linda Dano, who played flamboyant romance novelist Felicia Gallant, decided to get a face lift, she refreshingly came clean to the show and the press about her plans. "AW" addressed Dano's resulting bandages and changed appearance by having Felicia get caught in a fight between Alexander and Carl at a party, and crashing her through a spectacular skylight.

THE END: "AW," which was produced by P&G, was canceled to make room for the NBC-owned "Passions," which was supposed to make more money for the network since they owned it. "Passions" was created by former "Days" head writer James E. Reilly specifically to draw young (teenaged) eyeballs, which it did – but it never rose above last in the ratings. It was canceled in 2007.

"AW" focused its final episode on Cass and Lila's wedding, but gave the last word to Rachel. "All's well that ends well," she said to Carl, as the camera zoomed in on a photo of the still beloved Mac Cory.

Now that we've had a quick refresher course in these iconic soaps, let's look at what makes the entire genre so special, and so unique.

Buckle up!

CHAPTER 3
Soaps 101

How do soap operas WORK? You'll be surprised.

In the early days of television they were live of course, so whatever happened aired. Or not. The most famous - and infamous - event in live soap opera history occurred on November 22, 1963, the day President John F. Kennedy was shot. "As The World Turns" was airing, as usual. Bob Hughes had just told his mom Nancy that he had invited his ex-wife Lisa and their son Tom for Thanksgiving.

Ten minutes into the broadcast, CBS anchor Walter Cronkite interrupted, saying, *"Here is a bulletin from CBS News. In Dallas, Texas, three shots were fired at President Kennedy's motorcade in downtown Dallas. The first reports say that President Kennedy has been seriously wounded by this shooting. More details just arrived. These details about the same as previously: President Kennedy shot today just as his motorcade left downtown Dallas. Mrs. Kennedy jumped up and grabbed Mr. Kennedy, she called – 'Oh no!' and the motorcade sped on. United Press says that the wounds for President Kennedy perhaps could be fatal. Stay tuned to CBS News for further details."*

CBS then cut back to the soap. The actors had not been informed that the President had been shot, so they had kept acting throughout Walter Cronkite's announcement. A short while later, Cronkite came back on and continued reporting until it was confirmed President Kennedy was dead. This was all unbeknownst to the actors. They performed "As The World Turns" that day to its conclusion, at which point they were told the terrible news.

Fast forward to today, when soaps are taped 4-6 weeks in advance, so live interruptions are no longer a problem. But filming an hour (or even a half hour) of TV a day still presents huge, and often shocking, challenges.

ONE LIFE TO (TAPE) LIVE

For the record, a typical half-hour nighttime sitcom rehearses for a week, then tapes in front of a live audience on Friday night, stopping and starting over and over until they get it right. A typical one-hour soap tapes a full episode every day, stopping only if an actor drops dead.

I'm exaggerating, but not by much. The workload on a soap is greater than any other form of entertainment. It takes 10-15 writers to put five hours on TV every week. The head writer plots the long-term story for six months at a time. Breakdown writers parcel out the action episode by episode, leading slowly up to all the big events. Dialogue writers script the actual words the actors speak, including the classic lines fans have grown to love.

There are 5-7 directors on each show because it takes each director a week to plot out one episode. This is why the look sometimes changes from day to day, and why some episodes are moodier than others. It is the director's job to get all the work done in a regular Monday-Friday workday, because going overtime at night means BIG bucks. Most of the 200+ employees are union, and they get overtime. Directors who rack up a lot of overtime costs don't last very long on daytime.

Consequently, today's soaps have no time for rehearsal, so there is very little of it - save what the actors squeeze in on their own time in their dressing rooms. They don't stop tape unless an actor REALLY screws up, or the lighting/sound is unworkable.

For example, a few years ago, there was major construction going on near "One Life To Live's" 67th Street studio in Manhattan. The directors couldn't yell "cut" every time it happened, so the show worked laboriously to cover up the noise in the editing process. Once in a while, the sound of a jackhammer slipped through, though. The actors joked in interviews that there sure was a lot of construction in Llanview.

SETTING THE SCENE

As budgets got tighter in recent years, the first things to go were what shows hoped fans wouldn't notice, like scenery, clothing and extras. The fewer sets a show uses, the less money they spend. This means the writers have to build their stories around no more than two or three sets per episode.

This is why characters drop in on each other unannounced, and why so many members of the same family live together. Yes it heightens the drama, but it also saves money. And did you ever wonder why characters are always buying each other's homes? That's so the show can reuse the set, and even the furniture. That's also why there is only one jail cell, one courtroom, one coffee shop, one hotel room, etc. in town; and why there are only one or two bars and restaurants. It keeps costs down, besides guaranteeing that the main characters will run into each other to cause conflict and propel story.

The number of sets a character has is in direct correlation to how popular he or she is. Take "General Hospital's" Sonny Corinthos, for example. In 2011, he had a home living room set, a restaurant with a back office, and a house in the woods with a bedroom for trysts with Brenda.

Actors always feel more secure when their characters get their own "house." Few even get *bedrooms*, though. This is why so many characters have sex on the couch. "The

Young and the Restless" sex machines Nick and Phyllis did it
up against the wall, on the stairs, on the sofa, in the shower,
everywhere but a bed.

"We did have a bedroom set in the beginning, they
showed it a few times," clarifies Michelle Stafford, who plays
Phyllis. "But when [former exec] Lynn Latham left, they cut
the budget and started using fewer sets. That's when Nick and
Phyllis started having couch sex."

I often wondered why visitors were so eager to take a
seat on their couch, but, then again, Phyllis and Nick's guests
didn't see the shenanigans that we, the viewers, saw.

Most sets have staircases leading "upstairs" to unseen
bedrooms. A couple takes each other's hands and looks long-
ingly at each other as they ascend the stairs. The camera pans
away when they reach the top, because the stairs go nowhere.
The scarcity of sets has never applied to "The Bold and the
Beautiful's" Ridge and Brooke, however, who have both a
bedroom and a steam room for trysts. The money "B&B" has
invested in Ridge and Brooke's sex life shows in other areas,
though. Every patient in the local hospital stays in the exact
same hospital room.

The shows filmed in New York City have historically had a harder time changing sets, because their small studios don't have proper storage. They have had to store most of their sets and furniture outside the studio (like, in New Jersey). The crew then works all night long moving furniture in and out of the studio before taping resumes in the morning.

The LA-based shows have the luxury of more space, so they can store their sets on-site. The longest running permanent set I'm aware of was "General Hospital's" Nurses' Station, which was an immovable fixture on that stage for decades. You can almost still see Jessie Brewer in her crisp white nurse's uniform and navy cardigan comforting a patient or chastising an errant nurse from behind that commanding, raised perch.

Decorating a character's set is also up to the designers, but in some cases they infuse the space with real elements from the actor's life. "One Life To Live" did this with Commissioner Bo Buchanan's office at the police station. Robert S. Woods, who plays Bo, served as a Green Beret in Viet Nam, so the show wrote that history in years ago for Bo, as well. They asked Woods if they could have some photos from his time in the war when they designed Bo's office, and he com-

plied - so the framed photos of Bo in Viet Nam that currently

hang on the wall are real pictures of Bob Woods as a young

Green Beret.

DRESSED FOR EXCESS

It's easier to repurpose clothes than sets, but it's still a

challenge for the costume designer. Some fans complain that

characters repeat the same outfits, but I think it makes the

shows more real. Even rich people wear clothes more than

once. It *is* strange to see jewelry from one departed character

on another, but since there is only one jewelry store in town,

two people could technically be buying the same piece.

The costume designer is responsible for the look of

every character, every day. They shop for the main characters

a few times a year, keeping track of trends and the character's

place on the show. Rich characters wear better clothes, obvi-

ously.

Wardrobe keeps generic items like luggage, purses,

towels, prison jumpsuits, etc. on hand, too, but they have to

be careful how they recycle them, because soap fans are very observant.

"Guiding Light" Costume Designer Shawn Dudley learned this the hard way. "I used a robe on somebody once - I can't remember who - that had belonged to Tammy," Dudley recalls. "And we actually got a letter: 'Wow, I can't believe you used poor dead Tammy's robe on someone else.' It was a very non-descript robe. I couldn't believe someone noticed it!"

It was a running joke on "Guiding Light" that all the women in Springfield used the same Louis Vuitton suitcase when they packed in a huff. "[The execs] would say, 'Oh, the audience won't notice,'" recalls Dudley. "They noticed!"

Typically, the wardrobe room on a soap takes up the most space backstage. Clothes are divided by character, with jewelry, shoes, coats etc. to match. Every morning, the wardrobe dept. hangs that day's entire outfit in the actor's dressing room, including all of their jewelry - most notably wedding bands. Fans notice wedding rings more than anything else.

Actors often wear their real wedding bands since they aren't that noticeable, but actresses must stick with whatever bling they were gifted with during their big, splashy ceremonies. Former "As The World Turns" star Kelley Menighan

Hensley (Emily) often found real-life husband Jon Hensley's
(Holden) fake soap opera rings in their glove compartment.
He forgot to take "Holden's" ring off so often, the show had
to buy multiple bands for him. He'd notice his left hand on
the way home and then remove the ring(s) in the car.

"Take these back to the poor wardrobe people!" Kelley
would laugh.

NOT ALWAYS A BALL

Dressing 30+ contract players, plus that day's extras,
etc., is daunting enough, but imagine what happens when
a soap has to film a wedding, a New Year's Eve party, or a
costume ball. The actresses must all sport different colors
and stay in the same dress for weeks, because one event can
last on-air for a month. I remember one year when "All My
Children" was filming its annual Crystal Ball. They asked all
the actresses to come in for fittings to tailor their ball gowns.
One actress did not make time for this, and consequently
wound up in basic black. The other gals all showed up for
taping in stunning, brightly-colored gowns that hugged their
figures perfectly. The diva pitched a fit, but was reminded

that she had not made time for fittings. Drama ensued. The show solved it by cutting some of prettier-dressed women from the diva's scenes. Kelly Ripa (ex-Hayley) told me that she was asked to stay in her dressing room between scenes so as not to antagonize the diva in the halls with her gorgeous, fitted gown. That scenario is not surprising, because most actresses naturally want to be the prettiest in a large scene.

Wardrobe is also responsible for keeping actors looking good when they have put on a few pounds. There are sewing stations in every wardrobe room, which they use for everything from hemming to making clothes from scratch. They also have been known to take in and let out costumes, because actors and actresses fluctuate in weight just like "regular" people.

One East Coast actor gained and lost weight so frequently, the wardrobe people had three different sized pants for him at all times. Another famously difficult actress used to yell at the costume designer whenever her clothes didn't fit. Never mind that she gained about 30 pounds during the run of her show.

"You pick your battles," sighs the costume designer. "Some women when they get older are in denial. One actress just refused to admit she had grown out of a size 12 and started bringing in her own clothes. I did the best I could, but they were too tight and too young for her to be wearing. One day I got a call from production, 'Is [the actress] wearing her own clothes today?' 'Yup.' 'Got it.' Nobody wanted to fight with her."

That is very rare, though. Since a "day" on a soap can last for weeks, the show has to keep the outfits looking fresh every workday, cleaning and pressing them overnight or buying duplicates to make sure everyone looks their best. They are also adept at having actresses play pregnancy in real time, using a series of stomach pillows as the character's baby bump increases. Soap characters have the best maternity clothes on the planet, because wardrobe adjusts the outfits daily depending on how "far along" the character is.

The craziest day I ever saw in a wardrobe department occurred a few years back on "General Hospital," when three of their top female leads returned from a long holiday hiatus having gotten major breast implants, quite unbeknownst to the show. There was a mad scramble to alter their clothes in the short time before taping that day, never mind that the scenes on-air had to pick up from the "day before." It was quite noticeable to viewers that the women had, um, changed.

ACTING UP

The number of actors per scene and per show has changed, too. All actors are paid by the episode, so that is a logical place to cut the budget. Have you noticed the dwindling number of extras in "public places"? The lack of customers in restaurants, workers in offices, etc. has made soaps seem less real, but cutting them is better than cutting a main character.

Realism is relative on soaps, but they still strive for it. There are five levels of actors, all found, auditioned and hired by the casting department (the occasional exception applies to big stars and "soap hoppers," actors who call the Executive Producer for a job directly because they worked with them on a previous soap):

1) An extra appears in the background and makes $147 a day. This is the girl sipping coffee in the background,

the man getting out of the elevator, the passenger behind the
show's star on the airplane.

2) An "under-five" has fewer than five lines in an
episode and makes $405 a day. Examples would be the person
who takes a character's order, tells them their doctor is on line
one, says "Right this way, Mr. Quartermaine."

3) A recurring actor (or day player) makes more than
an under-five, but does not have a contract. The actor ne-
gotiates a day rate with the show, which is usually between
the union minimum of $931 and $1500, depending on their
status and length of service. This is the amount they are paid
for each episode on which they appear. (If they have an agent,
they are paid 10% more, which goes to the agent.)

In the old days, day players were the maid, butler and
secretary working for the local rich people, but that cost is
prohibitive today. Sorry, Dorian Lord, Stefano DiMera and
Victor Newman – you'll just have to answer your own doors
and telephones now.

"Many recurring day players are pivotal to story and
play major roles on the canvas," explains daytime's top casting
director Mark Teschner, who has been at "General Hospital"

for 21 years, winning three Daytime Emmys and five Artios Awards along the way. "Some of our most pivotal characters were recurring, but they appeared so much that the audience wasn't even aware they weren't under contract. Examples include the ongoing role of Anthony Zacchara played by Bruce Weitz (Mick Belker from "Hill Street Blues") the two-year run of Robert LaSardo as tattooed villain Manny, and the initial run of Sebastian Roche as Jerry Jacks. These are some of the most dynamic villains that have ever appeared on 'General Hospital.'"

Of course, not all major recurring roles are villains. Michael Learned (Olivia Walton from "The Waltons") played a three-month role as Shirley, a very uplifting cancer patient. Teschner adds that the casting of recurring players is often as important as contract roles.

"These are pivotal roles and I treat them seriously," he says. "Some very well known, recognizable actors appear in these roles and help elevate the storylines."

Indeed, Anthony Geary was hired in 1978 to play the short-term, recurring role of Bobbie Spencer's thuggish brother, Luke Spencer. The rest is soap opera history.

4) A guest star is someone like film actor James Franco, who drops into "General Hospital" to wreak havoc for a day or two when his schedule permits. He is paid per show... and did not have to audition.

5) A contract actor or "series regular" drives main story.

"It is not unusual for me to audition over 300 actors for one of these roles," reveals Teschner. "I am looking for that next star – the magic combination of charisma, sex appeal, potential and, most importantly, talent."

These actors have a written deal with the show guaranteeing them X amount of money per episode, and X number of episodes per contract cycle. A cycle could be 13, 26 or 52 weeks, depending on the clout of the actor. A contract newcomer can be let go after 13 weeks, but you can bet Susan Lucci's contract never came up for renewal more than once every two or three years.

Speaking of which, there was a lot of talk about Lucci taking a pay cut in the last year, which she admitted to Oprah Winfrey in February, 2011. I don't know the details of Lucci's contract, but I do know an actress of similar stature on another show who also took a cut - from $20,000 an episode to $15,000 an episode. This actress had a three show per week guarantee, which meant she went from $3.1 million a year to $2.3 million a year, working three days a week.

Don't cry for her, Argentina.

Another way soaps save money is by dropping contract actors to recurring, meaning they don't have to pay them for episodes not worked if they come in under their guarantee.

Let's use Jackie Zeman's aforementioned Bobbie as an example. As popular as she was during "General Hospital's" heyday in the 70s and 80s, she didn't work much after they killed Bobbie's husband Tony in 2006 - but "General Hospital" still had to meet Zeman's guarantee. So, the next time her contract came up, they dropped her to recurring. "General Hospital" can still write for Bobbie if they want, but they're not obligated. From a financial standpoint, it made more sense to give the job of head nurse to Epiphany, played by Sonya Eddy, because Eddy cost far less per day than Zeman, who has been with the show since 1977.

Casting is also responsible for casting babies and children. Back in the old days, an actress could convince a show to let them use her real-life baby. Hillary B. Smith did this with her baby son when her character Margo gave birth to Adam on "As The World Turns" in the 1980s. Katherine Kelly Lang's son Jeremy played Brooke's son Rick Forrester on "The Bold and the Beautiful" from 1990 to 1995.

But these days, a show can't stop tape when a baby isn't cooperating, so soap babies are actually played by twins or even triplets. There are strict laws about how long babies and children can be under the hot lights of a set, so it helps to have a spare or two.

AND THAT'S NOT ALL

Once a soap gets a handle on its crying babies, wardrobe malfunctions, and staircases to nowhere, they then have to schedule vacation and time off for the 30+ actors on the show. (Prime time doesn't have to do that; they film 22 shows a year with the whole cast and that's it.)

Ever wonder why "One Life To Live's" Viki is never on in early fall? That's because Erika Slezak has it in her contract that she gets a month-long vacation with her family in August. Every year, the writers have to come up with a reason why the heroine of their show will go missing. One year it was a road trip to Texas. Another year Viki visited her son in London. ("Have you heard from Mom?" one kid would ask another until she returned.)

Shows usually pre- and post-tape scenes with missing actors so that their absences won't be as noticeable. Typically, an actor tapes a series of one-way phone calls that the show can drop in throughout their time away.

Comas are another way to go. The actor films a bunch of scenes lying in a bed, and then the show builds the action around people talking about the poor coma patient at the foot of "their" bed, or by the hospital room door. The actor isn't even in the scene, but it sure looks like it on air.

"General Hospital" has developed Anthony Geary's absences into an art form. After over 30 years with the show, Geary has months off at a time, so Luke goes off on some caper or jewelry heist, checking in periodically with his loved ones. Fans have grown to expect Luke's crazy "schedule" and look forward to what the excuse will be this time.

"One Life To Live" does the same with Tuc Watkins, who plays David Vickers Buchanan by day on the soap, and Lynnette's gay lawyer Bob by night every Sunday on "Desperate Housewives." Since the shows tape 3000 miles away from each other, the New York-based soap will cram 40 scenes into two days for Watkins, which then air over a period of weeks. When the LA-based "Desperate Housewives" wraps for the season in April, Watkins returns to New York to tape the soap full-time, guaranteeing viewers they will see David through the summer.

"The Bold and the Beautiful" had to develop a similar schedule for Ronn Moss (Ridge), when he starred on Italy's version of "Dancing with the Stars" in 2010. "B&B" adjusted Moss's schedule so he would tape four shows in two days every Tuesday and Wednesday at the soap. He would then fly to Rome on Thursday, practice for and tape "DWTS" on Friday, Saturday and Sunday, and fly back to LA on Monday while studying his lines for the next week's "B&B" shows. This went on for 12 weeks (!) until he placed second and danced his way home.

And if you're wondering why Nikki went backburner in early 2011 on "The Young and the Restless," it's because Melody Thomas Scott needed back surgery. The show knew a few weeks in advance, so Nikki went to visit her off-screen sister, Casey.

Needless to say, actors are not allowed to call in sick to work on a daily soap opera. A show may throw in a line to explain a bad cold, or rewrite a scene so someone with the flu doesn't have to kiss their on-screen partner, but the soap must always go on.

MAKE UP TO BREAK UP

Luckily, the actors have a crack make-up and hair team to keep them looking their best. On a typical day, the actor hits the make-up chair for full frontal (face, chest, arms, hands) then switches over to the hair side of the room to get coiffed. This is definitely a perk.

But the actors don't always get to choose how they look. That's a decision made by the show for the character. And unless it's a new day in the soap action, their look must always be matched to how they looked the day before. The decision to go curly or straight must be discussed, because an actress like Laura Wright (Carly on "GH") may not want to spend an extra hour a day getting her hair blown straight for three straight weeks while Carly attends Sonny and Brenda's wedding.

The make-up artists take Polaroid pictures of the actors and then post them on the giant mirror in the make-up room, so that the next day's make-up people can match the look. This is always done for parties, balls, weddings, etc. when actresses have elaborate make-up and up-dos. It is also done when a character has been beaten up, shot, stabbed, had surgery, or been in an accident, because the wounds must match from day to day, and they must heal realistically. A black eye doesn't disappear overnight - it turns colors and fades.

The most difficult thing for actors is scars. Roger Howarth spent hours in the makeup chair getting Todd's facial scar applied every day on "One Life To Live." The predominance of characters who have had heart transplants means the daily application of chest scars, unless the show just doesn't care - as is the case with "GH's" Maxie. ("She had plastic surgery, so the scar doesn't show anymore," said a rep years ago. Um, okay.)

Tattoos are also a problem. If the actor has them, but the character doesn't, they must be carefully concealed with special, thick make-up. Usually, a show will try to write an actor's real tattoos in to the story, to avoid laborious time in the make-up chair. This is the case with the men of "General Hospital": Sonny, Nikolas and Dante have tattoos belonging to the actors who play them.

Conversely, if a character has a tattoo, it must be carefully applied. The most famous fake tattoos belong to "Days of our Lives" characters Bo Brady and John Black.

Bo's tattoo is a dagger that he got during the storyline that took him to Stockholm with Steve and Britta. John's is a Phoenix, which was a major plot point in 1986. When Marlena spied that tattoo on the amnesiac John, it made her think he might actually be Stefano DiMera with plastic surgery. He wasn't. John had the Phoenix tattoo "removed" in 2003, meaning Drake Hogestyn didn't have to spend so much time in the make-up chair anymore.

Some actors don't want a lot of make-up, like "The Young and the Restless's" Eric Braeden. Victor is a man's man, who has had to fight and scrape his way to the top in Genoa City. Braeden wants Victor to look real. Braeden is also the only actor to forbid *Soap Opera Digest* from retouching him in photographs. This includes the cover – HE wants to look real, too.

OH, BABY

You can't *conceive* of how difficult it is to write an actress's real-life pregnancy into a show. Soaps write up to six months ahead, so by the time an actress has confided her pregnancy to her boss, she is often showing. A scramble to cover her belly follows, until they figure out whether to write the pregnancy in, cover it up, put the character in a coma, or just send her away.

Fans are used to this. It's fun to read that so-and-so is pregnant in the soap magazines, and then watch how the show's writers deal with it. Will it be a sudden one-night stand? A sudden love of big purses?

"I was one of those girls who got pregnant and gained 70 pounds," recalled Kelly Ripa on "Live with Regis and Kelly." "I would say [to 'AMC'], 'How are you going to address it?' and they would say, 'We don't know.' At a certain point when I was pregnant with Michael, I got so big so quickly, they started out hiding me behind a big purse, then the sofa, then a door, then I was buried alive and held captive in a cave. Eventually, they buried me up to my neck. I did a lot of eye acting."

The best cover-up ever was on "As The World Turns" in 2002. Faced with all three of his leading ladies pregnant at the same time, head writer Hogan Sheffer concocted a crazy "evil spa" story that started with Carly (Maura West) disappearing from Oakdale. She woke up in a spa in Europe being slowly drugged, and was soon joined by Emily (Kelley Menighan Hensley) and Rose (Martha Byrne). The spa setting meant the women could wear giant white bathrobes, conveniently hiding their pregnancies. One by one, they vanished from the spa as the actresses had their babies and went on maternity leave.

A jealous Barbara was eventually revealed to be behind the revenge plot. Carly, Emily and Rose made their way home after the actresses had finished their leaves.

Still not impressed? Now imagine that your leading man just head-butted his onscreen rival, necessitating a trip to the hospital. Taping had to be stopped for the day.

Most people would be surprised at what goes on behind the scenes, too…

CHAPTER 4

Love of Life
(But Not Your Co-star)

What happens when co-stars don't like each other? Or don't like their story?

Again, you'd be surprised. Working with the same 200+ people every day in a small space gives each soap opera the feeling of a tight-knit family. A tight-knit, sometimes dysfunctional, family.

"Don't discount the effects of sunlight - or lack thereof - on the human mind," offers Hunt Block, who got his start as an extra on "Another World" and went on to work on five other soaps. (He was Lee Ramsey on "One Life to Live," Craig Montgomery on "As the World Turns," Guy Donahue on "All My Children," Ben Warren on "Guiding Light," and Peter Hollister on the nighttime soap "Knots Landing"). "Sometimes," offers Block, "it feels like working in an insane asylum on a submarine." Indeed, the New York soaps were notoriously dark, with many of the dressing rooms, make-up rooms and even sets constructed below street level with no windows. Block postures that the lack of fresh air and "inability to leave" contributed to some of the altercations he witnessed over the years - few of which fans ever knew about.

"There's no point in rehashing that," he says. "Besides, most people wouldn't believe it anyway."

Yeah…when tempers flare between co-stars, watch out. I remember one duo that absolutely despised each other. They were very popular, though, so the show would not split them up. The actor started eating garlic before their love scenes to get a rise out of his co-star. She kept her cool, but the situation grew too annoying. His antics resulted in them both being written off the show.

Most "super couples" are more professional than that. They recognize that the whole is greater than the sum of their (body) parts and make it work, even if they don't like each other. Readers of *Soap Opera Digest* were surprised to learn in a 1990 interview that "Days of our Lives" stars Peter Reckell and Kristian Alfonso, who had played Bo and Hope since 1983, had issues.

"When our storyline was big, we were together four to five days a week, 10 to 12 hours a day," said Reckell. "Yeah, we had our problems. But it was nothing out of the ordinary for two people who were working that closely all the time. Can't your temper flare every now and then? If not, you're not very human."

Trouble can also arise when the show splits a couple up, and moves them on to other partners.

"The only times we had problems with each other were when Bo and Hope were having problems with each other and we didn't have to work together," added Reckell. "That's where the tension comes from. But most of the time we have a formula. We're two people with fairly big egos, but even with those egos, we flow back and forth. It's a delicate balance and sometimes it gets jostled around a bit."

The press can impact that delicate balance, when one partner gets more attention (magazine covers, award nominations, personal appearances) than the other.

"We have different ideas on publicity, so we don't deal with each other outside of the studio," admitted Reckell. "We deal so much with each other in the studio, why get the rest all mixed up? Our relationship went through stuff and we've come out of it," Reckell summed up in a 1998 interview. "We've both grown up. We're more adult now and we're able to handle our emotions better."

Reckell and Alfonso both have spouses and kids and full lives away from the "Days" set, so they don't socialize a lot. But that doesn't matter to Bo and Hope's legion of fans. All they care about is that Bo and Hope look like they're in love on screen - and they do.

Sometimes, if the actors can't work it out like Reckell and Alfonso did, the show does break up a popular couple. In my experience, the biggest reason for this was when one person thought their partner was a bad actor and was bringing them down - or if their partner drank too much. Back in the 1980s and 90s, it was common for some actors to have a couple of drinks at lunch and then come back to work. This made the workday longer, and aggravated their sober co-stars. One popular couple on "Guiding Light" wound up splitting because he was abusive to her when he drank. She tried her best to "handle" him and just get through the day, but the Executive Producer broke them up anyway.

Actors request love interests, too. "All My Children's" Susan Lucci prefers tall co-stars, because her lighting is better. She and the 6'ft 3" Walt Willey (Jackson Montgomery) have been two-stepping for 20 years. Her co-star Michael Knight (Tad) became fast friends with Bobbie Eakes (Krystal) when she joined the show, so he pushed for a Tad/Kristal romance, and got it. And it has never worked when the show has tried to break up best friends Darnell Williams and Debbi Morgan (Jesse and Angie). They are so close, she asked him to give her away at her real-life wedding.

AS THE WORLD BURNS

The biggest lovefest of a cast I've ever seen was on "As The World Turns."

Lily (Martha Byrne) and Holden (Jon Hensley) were young love personified as the innocent heiress and the hunky stable boy in the 1980s. The actors did personal appearances together and became great friends. When Hensley left to try his luck in LA, Kelley Menighan had just joined the show as Emily. Menighan went on vacation to LA, and Byrne encouraged her to call Hensley for a drink. They dated, wed and currently have three kids - thanks to their co-star.

Next came good cop Jack (Michael Park) and conniving vixen Carly (Maura West) up through the super-couple ranks. Byrne, who was married by this point to a New York City Detective, would throw parties for the cast, who all grew closer. Maura West fell in love with Scott DeFreitas who played Andy Dixon, and they wed. Park married his high school sweetheart and the whole gang moved to the same upstate neighborhood where they threw barbecues and parties for each other. Some of them even wound up being godparents to each other's kids.

This is unusual, of course, but it illustrates how the family feeling of a soap can spill over into real life. The fans feel it, and become part of that family.

Like Byrne, many actors have been known to play matchmaker with their personal friends. "All My Children's" Cameron Mathison (Ryan) fixed up his best friend from Canada, Andrew Miller, with Eden Riegel, who played Bianca on the show. They wed in 2007 with Mathison in the wedding party, and recently had their first son.

And I was there when "All My Children's" Thorsten Kaye (Zach) introduced his on-screen love interest Alicia Minshew (Kendall) to his best friend Richie Herschenfeld at Herschenfeld's bar Prohibition in New York after the Daytime Emmys. Minshew and Herschenfeld started dating, and wed in 2008. They had a daughter in 2009.

Most spouses don't enjoy watching their loved ones make-out with their soap significant other, so they are careful not to tune in on major kissing days. This wasn't an option for "The Young and the Restless" Executive Producer Ed Scott, who spent decades watching his wife Melody Thomas Scott (Nikki) kiss Eric Braeden (Victor) from the production booth. It was all in a day's work for the no-nonsense Scott, though.

"Turn your face a little to the left," he would direct his wife, making sure her lighting was perfect while she kissed The Great Victor Newman.

JUST BE-CLAUSE

If an actor could get away with writing their preferences for co-stars and storylines into their contracts, they would. But the only instance of that actually being accomplished was Eileen Fulton's famous "Granny Clause" at "As the World Turns" in 1985, demanding that her character Lisa could not become a grandmother.

"I'm the only one who ever had the guts to have a 'Granny Clause,' and I did it for such a good reason," Fulton told *Soap Opera Digest*.

Fulton started thinking about it in the early 1970s, when Lisa's son Tom was rapidly aged to an adult and fell in love with Carol. Fulton had watched co-star Barbara Berjer (Claire) go through the same thing and become a young grandmother.

"Here she is looking so beautiful," recalled Fulton to NPR, "and suddenly they realized, 'My God, she's going to

be a great grandmother on our show! We have to kill her.'
So they hit her with a truck. I thought, 'That is not going to
happen to me.'"

Fulton went right to the source with her concerns.

"I called up Irna Phillips and said, 'So if Tom and
Carol have a baby, that makes me a grandmother.' She said,
'Yes, dear. That's the way soaps are. It's like life.' I said, 'Well,
I have a contract here and I'm not going to sign it until you
put in a 'Grandma Clause' saying that Tom and Carol will not
[have a baby].' So as time went on, poor Carol was sterile.
We called her Sterile Carol. Then Tom married Natalie and
she couldn't have any babies either, because she had some
kind of disease. She died."

"Later on, in the 80s, Lisa was certainly old enough to
be a grandmother, though she was having wild affairs. When
Tom and Margo were going to have a baby, they had them
lose the baby in a gunfight. It was awful. People still remembered I had a 'Grandma Clause.' I got hate mail from everywhere saying, 'You son of a … we're going to kill you. We're
going to fix it so you'll never act again.' So I had to have a
bodyguard."

Surprised by all the fuss - "It was just a foam rubber
pillow!" - Fulton eventually gave up the clause, and Tom and
Margo had a son, Casey. He was soon rapidly aged, of course.

NO FIGHTING, NO BUTTING

The story of Eric Braeden (Victor) and Peter Bergman's (Jack) backstage altercation in 1991 is old news now,
but it did shake up "The Young and the Restless" for a while
back in the day. The story as I heard it from people who
were there was that Braeden cut his own dialogue in a scene,
which he often did. Braeden informed the director he was
doing that, but the director neglected to tell Bergman. So,
when they were filming the scene and Bergman didn't get
the cue he was expecting, he made a disparaging comment to
Braeden. (I heard that the comment was, "Learn your lines,
old man.") An argument ensued that carried into a dressing
room, where Braeden head-butted Bergman, requiring a trip
to the hospital and stitches for Bergman.

Boss Bill Bell was NOT pleased, and he came down
hard. Apologies were offered, the press was told to lay off,
and "Y&R" went back to business as usual. To both Braeden

and Bergman's credit, they have forged a respectful working relationship in the 20 years since that incident, both receiving Emmy Awards and accolades in the process. They still may not like each other, but you'd never know it from watching their work, or from the way they compliment each other in the press now. They line up every year for the annual "Y&R" cast photo, smiling broadly in their tuxedoes.

One big happy family.

I never got to watch "Guiding Light" very much while I was working, but I remember one lady at the cardiology clinic noticed me looking at "GL" on her TV and said, "Oh, honey, do you watch this story?" I said yes. She held my hand and said, "Just sit on my bed and watch the last ten minutes with me, will you?" It was in the line of duty. I remember Jennifer was on the stand about to reveal that she was Amanda's mother.

My grandmother who lived 100 miles away would make me audiotapes of "GL," adding in little tidbits I needed to know. She'd mail the tapes to me every Friday afternoon, and every Saturday I'd listen to five hours of "GL." I loved that show. I started watching when Rita was married to Ed Bauer but carryin' on with Alan Spaulding. And Roger Thorpe! He was one of daytime's most complex and intriguing characters. Then they killed Maureen Bauer. I can still see her and Ed in their kitchen after she found out about his affair with Lillian. She said, "You have broken my heart." And then Maureen was gone.

I watched all my soaps – "AMC," "OLTL" and "GL" -- when I was in labor with my son Joel. I remember that Nola was on and I got my way with the remote. My son Tom was born on a Sunday, very considerate, that one.

Later I got into "Y&R" when we got a VCR. As soon as I heard that Sears had them, I put the kids in their car seats and off we went. It was amazing, and it also worked for cartoons. Those were the best days of my life.

- Marcia Mills from Arkansas

CHAPTER 5
Only on Soap Operas

"A soap opera is kind of a sandwich," wrote humorist James Thurber in a 1948 article for *The New Yorker* called O PIONEERS, "whose recipe is simple enough, although it took years to compound. Between thick slices of advertising, spread 12 minutes of dialogue, add predicament, villainy, and female suffering in equal measure, throw in a dash of nobility, sprinkle with tears, season with organ music, cover with a rich announcer sauce and serve five times a week."

Thurber was talking about the 15-minute radio soaps of the day, but the recipe is the same today.

"That's a pretty concise description," agrees famed author Peter Straub of Thurber's take on soaps. The award-winning Straub, who wrote *Ghost Story*, *Koko*, and *The Talisman* (with Stephen King) among many other titles, is a longtime fan of "All My Children" and "One Life To Live." He has even appeared on "One Life To Live" as the former partner of John McBain's late father - a blind cop who nevertheless sees all.

I turned to Straub for his take on soaps because as a famous, married Manhattan author he would not be considered your typical soap fan, yet soaps hold great value to him. (And also because I missed interviewing James Thurber by about 40 years.)

"Soap operas are a surefire, faithful source of sheer innocent narrative pleasure," offers Straub. "Storyline with a capital S, where every line of dialogue helps propel some part of a plot."

He cites Luna Moody, a character on "One Life To Live" in the 90s, as an example of the "sheer pleasure" soaps have brought him and millions of other viewers through the years.

"Luna had this feel-good radio program," he recalls. "You could feel her voice going through the town bringing peace and enjoyment to all her listeners, which is what soap operas do. Todd Manning is an amoral millionaire capable of whipping up a thousand intrigues over lunch. There's an amazing amount of tension rolling through every soap opera scene, even if it's just two women with fabulous hair doing nothing but talking to each other."

Straub agrees that one of the most entertaining elements of soaps is how they embrace their conventions full-on. Nothing is too far-fetched or outrageous if it propels a story.

"The minute a baby is born, you know that their DNA has been messed with," laughs Straub. "When you see a guy walking around in a towel, you know that towel is going to fall and the girls are going to go, 'Oooh!' Any time someone is behind a steering wheel, that car is going to crash."

As a novelist, Straub especially appreciates the darker side of characters that soaps are able to explore.

"All these stories about evil twins and split personalities speak to certain realities that soap operas put right up front. Most people are aware that there is some kind of nighttime self inside them; in their adolescent years, that person was driving the car. I have such an entity. That person inside evokes all kind of feelings, primarily suspense. That's the raw material of soap operas. It's Dickensian. Charles Dickens could have written these stories today."

Dickens certainly pioneered them, parceling out *Great Expectations* in serial form from 1860 to 1861, keeping his readers coming back every week to see what happened.

Sound familiar?

"A loving heart is the truest wisdom," wrote Dickens.

Except on soap operas, where a loving heart usually means that a woman will change a paternity test to keep her husband from finding out that she slept with his brother while trapped in a rainstorm nine months ago when she thought her husband was dead...

Lead on, Spirit!

CONVENTION-AL WISDOM

Here are a few of the conventions and okay, clichés, we have come to expect from our favorite shows. Make sure you read this dressed in a ball gown, in full makeup and hair, drinking bourbon out of a crystal glass that you poured from a decanter.

THE CLIFFHANGER

Perfected by Irna Phillips, soaps would not be complete without the reveal, the close-up, then the cut to commercial. Here are two examples from the April 1, 2011 episode of "One Life To Live":

> *Charlie (to Echo in bed): "As soon as the custody case is over, I'm going to tell [wife] Viki about us. No more secrets, no more hiding, no more worrying that she is going to find out about us the wrong way."*
>
> *Motel room door opens: Viki enters, horrified. Music swells.*
>
> *Cut to:*
>
> *Clint: "No, it wasn't you. You didn't kill Eddie Ford."*
> *Nora: "Then who did, Clint?"*

Clint: "Your son. (Camera zooms in.) Matthew shot Eddie Ford."

Music crescendos. Fade to black.

Like that.

SORAS

"Soap Opera Rapid Aging Syndrome" is a term coined by former *Soap Opera Weekly* editor Mimi Torchin that has caught on and become part of the lexicon. The term applies to pretty much all soap children who are sent to the other room or boarding school between the ages of toddler and teen because of the strict laws governing the hours a child actor can work, the need for a tutor on set, etc. Whenever a child is sent away to visit a relative, attend school, or even just take a vacation; you can bet he or she will return as a gorgeous teen with a chip on their shoulder - SORAS'd.

THE SECRET

Every new character is hiding something. Even if the show doesn't know what it is, they tell the actor to play it anyway.

"I remember when I was on 'One Life,' they told me at the end of a scene, 'Look over your shoulder. You have a secret,'" reveals Thorsten Kaye, who played dreamy poet Patrick Thornhart on the show in the 90s. "I said, 'What secret? What am I hiding?' They said, 'We can't tell you.'"

NO LOCKED DOORS

Doors are never locked on soaps because people need to walk in on nefarious dealings they shouldn't be seeing. If a door is locked, then the person inside the room will open the door to the wrong person thinking it's someone else. "What, did you forget your key?" is the standard line for the person inside to yell as they open the door to the ex-husband, lover, serial killer, the exact person they are trying to avoid. *Note: This also explains why characters never carry keys or purses. (Unless they are hiding a real-life pregnancy and need a big purse to cover their belly.)*

THE INTERRUPTED WEDDING

No daytime wedding goes off without a hitch. When

the minister says "If there is anyone here who can provide just cause why these two should not be joined, speak now or forever hold your peace," it's a guarantee that an ex will come back from the dead to burst into the church. At the very least, the bride will be busted for kissing someone else the night before, or the sprinkler system will go off.

DADS R'nt US

The baby is rarely fathered by the husband. The baby is usually fathered by a relative or best friend of the husband. A DNA test will be conducted to prove who the father is, which, as Peter Straub points out, will be altered 100% of the time. There is no point in conducting a DNA test if it's *not* going to be altered.

NO BODILY FUNCTIONS

No one ever has to go to the bathroom on soaps, including people tied up or locked in a cage in the basement. If a woman is shown going into the bathroom, there will be a catfight in the bathroom. Men never have fights in bathrooms, because the shows don't want to show urinals.

NO MONEY

Characters never carry money. When they eat out, no bill arrives at the table. No money is exchanged for drinks at bars. If a wallet is shown, that means it will either be stolen, or something will fall out of it that the character is hiding.

MUSIC MONTAGES

If a couple is really in love, they get a music montage, which plays while they "make love." The camera will shoot them from every angle while carefully avoiding all major body parts. If they're in it for the long haul, they get their own song. "General Hospital's" Jason and Sam don't even hold hands without Rie Sinclair's "Just You and Me" playing in the background.

TALKING ALOUD

Characters talk to themselves for two reasons, both of which indicate lazy writing.

1) The writers need to recap a plot point. "Days of our Lives" has been the biggest offender of this over the years. Numerous times per episode, a character can be found saying,

"I sure hope my husband doesn't find out the baby isn't his!"
to make sure the audience knows the baby isn't her husband's.

"All My Children" recently showcased one of the
worst I've ever seen: Murderer Ricky had a whole monologue
talking to the newspaper clipping of the girl he murdered,
saying he was going to get engaged to Kendall and "make her
love me." The newspaper did not respond.

2) Someone needs to overhear a secret.

"I sure hope so-and-so doesn't find out I'm pregnant!"
says a girl out loud to herself as that exact person listens.

NO ONE EATS

There is no food unless it is about to be thrown, or
if the meal will be interrupted. Kitchen sets are rarely used,
unless someone needs to express their frustration by noisily
getting a beer out of fridge or having a food fight.

And NO ONE grocery shops. The only time I ever
saw someone using a shopping cart in a supermarket, it was
the Chandler housekeeper on "All My Children" buying the
peanut butter that Dixie inexplicably asked to be served on
her pancakes so she could be poisoned to death by accident by

the Satin Slayer.

DOPPELGANGERS

Lookalikes pop up most often when the show has killed a character, but then wants to bring the actor back. On "All My Children" we had Kitty/Kelly, Jesse/Jacob, Cindy/Karen and Tad/Ted. The other reason is to show off an actor's talent, like "AMC's" David Canary playing Adam Chandler and his twin brother Stuart concurrently for 25 years, which won him five Emmys.

"Days of our Lives" recently wrote a story where FBI agent Rafe was kidnapped by Stefano, who then slotted a plastic surgery'd version of Rafe into his life. No one noticed, including Rafe's loving bride Sami.

Which leads to another soap staple…

DOPPELGANGER SEX

Soap characters never notice when their loved one has been replaced. Not even in bed, which begs the question… does everyone on soaps have sex the exact same way? "Days's" Rafe and Faux Rafe sure did, because Sami wasn't suspicious of him for weeks, and they were doing it on the couch regularly.

Ditto for "B&B's" Brooke, who lead her masked husband Ridge outside at her daughter's graduation party for some hot sex against the wall of the house – or so she thought. Ooops! It was her daughter's young boyfriend, Oliver, wearing Ridge's jacket - which begs the question, what is Ridge's exercise routine that Brooke couldn't tell her 50 year-old husband from an 18 year-old boy?

Brooke didn't figure out her mistake until days later when she commented to Ridge about how awesome and "different" their mask sex had been. "What are you talking about?" responded Ridge.

"Gulp."

COURTROOM ANTICS

The person tried is never the person who did it, and the defendant is never quiet. Whenever a witness says something the defendant disagrees with, they jump up and scream, "That's not true!" The courtroom erupts, and the judge pounds his/her gavel, yelling, "Order in the court!"

When the wrong person is inevitably found guilty, they jump bail. "Y&R's" Sharon was found guilty of pushing Skye into a Hawaiian volcano, so she ran to the courthouse bathroom, knocked out a guard, managed to dislodge the metal bars on the window and climbed her way out the window to freedom.

In four-inch heels, of course.

NO WEATHER

Weather has no impact, unless it's a hurricane, tornado, rainstorm or blizzard in which two people will get trapped and inevitably have sex. Women's clothes do not change with the seasons. They go sleeveless all winter long, and always sport stilettos or strappy sandals regardless of the time of year or activity. Erica Kane was recently held hostage in a locked room and kept her high heels on the whole time.

The young hunky guys walk around in towels all year long. If they are working out at the local gym, they will play the next three episodes still in their workout clothes, even if it's snowing – and they're outside.

EVERY TOWN HAS A MENTAL WARD

Even the smallest soap towns have mental institu-
tions. "Y&R" attached its rubber rooms to the town's regular
hospital, so nutbags like Sheila, Patty and Daisy could roam
the halls as they pleased.

ABC likes to name its loony bins. "One Life To
Live's" Viki, Jessica, Addie, Hannah and Marty have all done
time in St. Anne's, while poor Annie on "All My Children"
had her own wing at Oak Haven. "General Hospital's" Laura
slipped into a catatonic state when she remembered having
killed Rick Webber, so Luke had to ship her off to Shadybrook. Crazy Lisa spent only 24 hours in Shadybrook after
trying to kill Robin before she was released to go back to *practice medicine*, so "GH's" nuthouse is clearly the most efficient
of the bunch.

NO ONE EVER DIES IN A PLANE CRASH

People either survive the crash, or the body isn't
found. "AMC's" Zach went down in the ocean, but his
suitcase washed up on shore, a clear sign that he survived.
"B&B's" Brooke and Thomas crashed into the ocean off Fiji,

but luckily, he was able to give her CPR on a broken piece of the plane while still in the water. They washed up together on an island in strategically torn clothing.

The only character I can recall dying on an airplane was "Days's" Shawn Brady. He had a heart attack.

ELEVATORS = SEX

Any time a character enters an elevator, it will get stuck. If its two characters, they will either fight, have sex, or one will deliver the other's baby. "Y&R's" Victor and Skye struck up an unholy alliance while trapped. "AMC's" Erica met Travis in a stuck elevator, leading to two marriages and the birth of Bianca. "ATWT's" Luke and Reid fell in love between floors. Sonny and Carly got trapped together on New Year's Eve 1999, forcing him to admit he's claustrophobic and drawing them closer before the millennium.

But mostly, characters have sex. If you don't believe me, check out the YouTube video called "DOOL - What To Do When Trapped In An Elevator" starring "Days" duos Chloe and Lucas, and EJ and Nicole hotly disrobing to the tune of Aerosmith's "Love in an Elevator."

Even if Steven Tyler isn't a soap fan, he would be down with that.

SHORT SUPERMODELS

Only on daytime do short, tiny girls become famous models. "AMC's" Erica is the gold standard. She is barely five feet and has been a supermodel and spokeswoman for about four decades. All the Fusion girls who work for her have been models, which could be more of a comment on Erica wanting to save money than on the logic of hiring short executives to sell clothing and cosmetics. "GH's" Brenda, "Y&R's" Lily, "B&B's" Brooke; every show has a vertically challenged girl making big bucks to model in a small town.

SWEET MOBSTERS

Soap mobsters don't deal in drugs or prostitution. They love children and pets. They plan romantic evenings and vacations for their women. They only kill bad guys, and even then, it's usually off screen.

"GH's" Sonny never lets his business as a "coffee importer" get in the way of being there for his kids or planning candlelight dinners for Brenda. And he never orders a hit. He just tells Jason to "take care of it," and goes back to laying rose petals on the bed for his beloved.

BABYNAPPING NANNIES

If the nanny is a day player hired to take a soap child out of the room, it's fine. But if the nanny is a contract player, she will absolutely kidnap the child. The minute "Y&R's" Billy and Victoria hired Kevin's nutty ex-wife Jana to care for their new baby Lucy, you knew it was going to go horribly wrong. Not only did Jana kidnap Lucy, she took Chloe's toddler Delia along, too.

RILING UP KIDS

Because we rarely see characters' children on soaps, the actors playing the parents tend to go overboard in scenes with the kids when they are shown together. A real dad would be trying to calm his kid down at bedtime, but "AMC's" Ryan throws Emma over his shoulder and tickles the poor over-stimulated kid every time he takes her upstairs to "bed." Kendall is always playing tickle monster with her boys and loudly poking them.

Which is ironic because one of them is *deaf.*

"ATWT's" Margo used to run after her kids at bedtime with such fake frivolity that *I* couldn't sleep. The constant goofing around actually makes the scenes seem less
realistic, because real parents would never do that. The actor
should just put their arm around the little day player toddler
du jour and say the lines.

DON'T GO UPSTAIRS

We've already established that soap staircases go nowhere, but there's another reason not to ascend all the way to
the top: you might never come down.

The funniest and most-inside joke regarding "going upstairs" involves "AMC's" Bobby Martin. The son of
Joe Martin was sent upstairs in 1970 to "polish his skis" and
was never heard from again. Years later, "AMC" winked at
the audience by having Opal get locked in the Martin's attic
and stumbling onto a skeleton sporting a ski cap that read
"Bobby." Another time, Jake referred to a Halloween skeleton
decorating Myrtle's boarding house as his "older brother."

DYING IS RELATIVE

Even when a character dies on screen, they can always come back. Maybe they were whisked away by Witness Protection. Maybe their heart started pumping again in the morgue. Maybe they had a twin we/they didn't know about (as we've discussed). We can even *watch* them die and go to heaven, where their loved ones will encourage them to come back to earth, and yet they still live. Disturbingly, sometimes the ghosts of the heavenly loved ones are played by plastic surgery'd versions of other actors who left the soap and never found work.

That's been a cautionary tale for actors since soap operas started on television – should a young actor take the leap to primetime and film, and risk not working? Or stay on the soap where the paycheck and work is steady?

No one is ever REALLY dead - unless the actor makes the big time.

CHAPTER 6

Six Degrees

ost people would be shocked by all the famous actors who got their start on soaps. But to soap fans, the MOST famous actors are the ones who stay working in Daytime.

"It always bothers me when someone says soaps are a great 'training ground,'" says Rena Sofer, who played Rocky on "Loving" and Lois on "General Hospital," for which she won an Emmy. Sofer went on to major roles on "Heroes," "Ed," "24," and "NCIS" among many others.

"Soaps are hard work," she asserts. "The trick for young actors is to keep it about the work, and not get caught up in their own press, or the money. Those that can do that can stay fulfilled on a soap for years. There's no better job for a working mom than being on a soap opera."

In fact, some actresses, like Susan Lucci and Erika Slezak, wrote it in to their contracts that they must be home when their kids got home from school, and off for their kids' school vacations.

"The reason I don't like to use the phrase 'training ground' is because of people like Susan and Erika," continues Sofer. "I think it is insulting to their life's work and their choice of medium to refer to it as *just* that. Just a training ground. To them, this is their pinnacle - and to say that their medium's purpose is simply to 'train' is wrong."

Personally, I find it ignorant when non-soap fans talk about actors who stayed in daytime not "making it." In what universe would two women like Lucci and Slezak, who have been working actresses for over 40 years, raised families with the same husbands for almost as long, and made over $50 million each, be considered failures?

"People leave because they want to be challenged," offers Thorsten Kaye, who earned his Masters degree in classical theatre and started his PhD in between stints on "One Life To Live," "Port Charles" and "All My Children."

"Erika Slezak has been challenged, that's why she stayed as long as she has. With Lucci, you've watched a bad character find her way to redemption. Most actors can't count on that on a yearly basis, but those two can. I think a lot of people leave because they want to do something else. There's nothing wrong with that. Just as there's nothing wrong with people who find soaps challenging and choose to stick around."

Let's play six degrees of famous people who began their careers on soaps, starting with - who else? - Kevin Bacon.

THEY STARTED ON SOAPS

Kevin Bacon, "Search for Tomorrow" and "Guiding Light"

Christina Applegate, "Days of our Lives"

Richard Dean Anderson, "General Hospital"

Armand Assante, "The Doctors"

Alec Baldwin, "The Doctors"

Christine Baranski, "Another World"

Angela Bassett, "Ryan's Hope"

Kathy Bates, "All My Children" and "The Doctors"

Warren Beatty, "Love of Life"

Maria Bello, "Ryan's Hope"

Robby Benson, "Search for Tomorrow"

Tom Berenger, "One Life To Live"

Halle Berry, "Knots Landing"

Jason Biggs, "As The World Turns"

Yasmine Bleeth, "Ryan's Hope" and "One Life To Live"

Jordanna Brewster, "As The World Turns"

Amy Carlson, "Another World"

Tia Carrere, "General Hospital"

Dixie Carter, "Edge of Night"

Lacey Chabert, "All My Children"

Eddie Cibrian, "The Young and the Restless" and "Sunset Beach"

Margaret Colin, "As The World Turns"

Courteney Cox, "As The World Turns"

Marcia Cross, "One Life to Live"

Ted Danson, "Somerset"

Kim Delaney, "All My Children"

Dana Delany, "Love of Life" and "As The World Turns"

Robert DeNiro, "Search for Tomorrow"

Leonardo DiCaprio, "Santa Barbara"

Taye Diggs, "Guiding Light"

Josh Duhamel, "All My Children"

Olympia Dukakis, "Search for Tomorrow"

Kirsten Dunst, "Loving"

Charles Durning, "Another World"

Christine Ebersole, "One Life To Live"

Morgan Fairchild, "Guiding Light" and "Search for Tomorrow"

William Fichtner, "As The World Turns"

Nathan Fillion, "One Life To Live"

Calista Flockhart, "Guiding Light"

Michelle Forbes, "Guiding Light"

Faith Ford, "Another World" and "One Life To Live"

Vivica A. Fox, "Generations" and "The Young and the Restless"

Morgan Freeman, "Another World"

Sarah Michelle Gellar, "All My Children"

Kelsey Grammer, "Another World"

Mark Hamill, "General Hospital"

Jackee Harry, "Another World"

David Hasselhoff, "The Young and the Restless"

Teri Hatcher, "Capitol"

Anne Heche, "Another World"

Marg Helgenberger, "Ryan's Hope"

Lauryn Hill, "As The World Turns"

Dustin Hoffman, "Search for Tomorrow"

Lauren Holly, "All My Children"

Kate Jackson, "Dark Shadows"

Allison Janney, "Guiding Light"

James Earl Jones, "As The World Turns"

Tommy Lee Jones, "One Life To Live"

Melina Kanakaredes, "Guiding Light"

Harvey Keitel, "Dark Shadows"

Kevin Kline, "Search for Tomorrow"

Jane Krakowski, "Search for Tomorrow"

Joe Lando, "One Life To Live" and "Guiding Light"

Eva LaRue, "All My Children"

Melissa Leo, "All My Children"

Judith Light, "One Life To Live"

Ray Liotta, "Another World"

Nia Long, "Guiding Light"

Eva Longoria, "The Young and the Restless"

Ricky Martin, "General Hospital"

Rue McClanahan, "Another World"

Bette Midler, "Edge of Night"

Demi Moore, "General Hospital"

Julianne Moore, "As The World Turns"

Shemar Moore, "The Young and the Restless"

Matthew Morrison, "As The World Turns"

Kate Mulgrew, "Ryan's Hope"

Ming Na Wen, "As The World Turns"

Leonard Nimoy, "General Hospital"

Chris Noth, "Another World"

Hayden Panettiere, "One Life to Live" and "Guiding Light"

Luke Perry, "Loving"

Ryan Phillippe, "One Life To Live"

Brad Pitt, "Another World"

Parker Posey, "As The World Turns"

Sara Ramirez, "As The World Turns"

Christopher Reeve, "Love Of Life"

Ving Rhames, "Another World"

Kelly Ripa, "All My Children"

Charlotte Ross, "Days of our Lives"

Brandon Routh, "One Life to Live"

Meg Ryan, "As The World Turns"

Susan Sarandon, "Search for Tomorrow" and "A World Apart"

Tom Selleck, "The Young and the Restless"

Amanda Seyfried, "All My Children"

Ted Shackelford, "Another World"

Charles Shaughnessy, "Days of our Lives"

Martin Sheen, "Edge of Night"

Gary Sinise, "Knots Landing"

Christian Slater, "Ryan's Hope"

Wesley Snipes, "All My Children"

Brittany Snow, "Guiding Light"

Rena Sofer, "Loving" and "General Hospital"

John Stamos, "General Hospital"

Susan Sullivan, "Another World"

Michelle Trachtenberg, "All My Children"

John Travolta, "Edge of Night"

Janine Turner, "General Hospital"

Tamara Tunie, "As The World Turns"

Blair Underwood, "One Life To Live"

Christopher Walken, "Guiding Light"

Cynthia Watros, "Guiding Light"

Michael Weatherly, "Loving"

Sigourney Weaver, "Somerset"

Jo Beth Williams, "Somerset"

Robin Wright, "Santa Barbara"

Obviously, these actors found great fame and fortune after soaps, but some of them also found great heartache. I bet some of them wish they had stayed, banking good money and being part of a real family for 10, 20, 30, 40 years.

I honestly don't recall a time in my life when I didn't watch soaps. My whole family was full of ABC Daytime diehards and my mom watched the entire lineup, from "Ryan's Hope" to "Edge of Night." The stories that hooked me were the love story of Jesse and Angie on "AMC" and "GH's" Ice Princess story. We weren't used to seeing black peeps on daytime so to have a middle class black family represented (years before Cosby) resonated with us. Angie and Jesse were OUR Luke and Laura.

At one point or another, I have watched every soap. I have a niece named Brittany Eden after Sharon Gabet's character on "Another World" and Marcy Walker's on "Santa Barbara." My best friend's mom and my mom can't stand each other, so we call them Viki and Dorian.

There's a group of women and men in my office who watch "One Life to Live" every day at work. The show respects its history, has multi-generational storytelling and the dialogue is phenomenal. With the exception of the Stacy debacle a few years back, very little of what "OLTL" does disappoints me.

I truly feel like I've lost friends with its cancellation.

- **Dave Jordan from Brooklyn NY**

CHAPTER 7
Black To The Future

In the early days, the problem with integrating non-white characters into a soap was that a large segment of the audience did not want to see interracial dating. So you had an entirely white canvas with a suddenly added non-white family or character. Who were they going to date? Audiences rejected the most benign interaction.

Even the great Irna Phillips couldn't make it work when she paired the Eurasian Mia Elliott with American Viet Nam war pilot Paul Bradley on "Love Is A Many Splendored Thing" in the late 1960s. As outlined in an earlier chapter,

CBS exec Fred Silverman pronounced the story too controversial and ordered Phillips to kill it. She refused, and quit.

Having learned from Irna Phillips' experiences, Agnes Nixon and Bill Bell included black characters at the outset of their new shows, to try and insure that they would be an integral part of the canvas. Nixon tackled race relations right out of the gate on the first soap she created, "One Life To Live." Carla Benari was introduced as an Italian-American who went to work as Dr. Jim Craig's receptionist. Carla soon started dating a black intern named Dr. Price Trainor, which prompted angry letters from viewers about a white woman dating a black man.

About six months later, it was revealed that Carla was actually Llanview Hospital Housekeeper Sadie Gray's daughter.

She was a black woman passing as white.

Agnes Nixon then turned the story on its head, by having Jim Craig fall for Carla, bringing Round Two of angry letters, this time for uniting a white man and a black woman - the same woman, mind you.

Carla eventually revealed herself to Jim, who proposed anyway. She then came out as a black woman to all of Llanview and became a major player in a number of stories through the 1970s. Although some southern ABC affiliates dropped the soap because of Carla's controversial story, it put "One Life To Live" on the map. The show had a 5.4 rating in 1969, but had shot up to an 8.2 by 1973. (A Nielsen ratings point equaled 874,000 homes back then.)

As for Bill Bell, he decided simply to write a black romance equal to how he would write a white romance. Tyrone Jackson and Amy Lewis were a young couple in love in 1984. They were also black, but Bell gave them the same moody montages and sexy love scenes that his white couples got. Taking a page from Agnes Nixon's Carla, Bell gave Tyrone a story where he had to disguise himself as white to take down an organized crime figure. He infiltrated the mob by posing as a white man named Robert and romancing The Don's daughter, Alana. Tyrone revealed himself as a black man to Alana after her father was killed, but like "One Life To Live's" Jim Craig, Alana said the color of his skin didn't matter. Tyrone was not in love with Alana though, and he reconciled with Amy.

Note: Tyrone was played by Phil Morris, who went on to play Kramer's fast talking lawyer Jackie Chiles on "Seinfeld." Amy was played by Stephanie E. Williams, who was later "General Hospital's" Simone Hardy.

Bell also introduced Abbott family housekeeper Mamie Johnson in the 1980s, cleverly positioning her as the wise sage who raised the Abbott children after their horrible mother Dina abandoned them. When patriarch John Abbott got remarried to scheming Jill, Mamie was the one who foiled her plots and kept peace in the house.

But you're no one without a family on soaps, so in 1990, Bell gave Mamie two nieces. Drucilla and Olivia Barber joined the show and eventually married half brothers Neil and Malcolm Winters, creating a core family that continues to this day.

Victoria Rowell, who played Drucilla, left the show in 2007 after some choppy years during which she didn't feel that African American actresses, including her, were getting a fair shake. After the aforementioned Stephanie Williams joined "General Hospital" as Simone, she found herself in a controversial story where Simone and her white husband, Dr.

Tom Hardy, had a baby that could have also been fathered

by Simone's black lover, Dr. Harrison Davis. Paternity tests

revealed Dr. Davis was the father. He sued for custody on

the grounds that a black child should have two black parents,

which brought up interesting questions of racial identity

and prejudice - and is an argument that still resonates today

within the black community. However, it was later proven

that Harrison had forged the test results. (Naturally.) Simone

and Tom were reunited with their son Tom Hardy, Jr., and

Harrison was fired by the baby's grandfather, famed "GH" Dr.

Steve Hardy.

BLACK LIKE THEE

"All My Children" has had the best success of all, with

Angie (Debbi Morgan) and Jesse Hubbard (Darnell Wil-

liams), who became soaps' first black super couple in 1982.

The Hubbards remain popular and frontburner, but it's been a

rocky road.

Williams elected to leave the show in 1988, so the

show killed his character. Angie turned to Cliff Warner as she mourned Jesse. Angie and Cliff had also just lost their close friend Cindy Chandler to AIDS.

(Note: Cindy was played by Ellen Wheeler, who became a director and would go on to play a major role in the death of "Guiding Light" as its Executive Producer.)

Angie and Cliff, who was white (and played by Peter Bergman, now Jack Abbott on "The Young and the Restless"), fell in love and got engaged. But "All My Children" backed away from telling a full-on interracial love story, which angered Morgan. She quit "All My Children" in 1990 to join the new, more racially diversified soap, "Generations" as Chantal.

"Generations" was a noble experiment that aired on NBC from March, 1989 to January, 1991. It was the first soap to feature a core African-American family from day one, and the first to show black and white families enjoying equal status and prosperity. The show propelled the careers of Vivica A. Fox, Kelly Rutherford (Lily, "Gossip Girl"), and Kristoff St. John, who has played Neil Winters on "The Young and the Restless" since 1992.

But "Generations" never rose above the bottom in the ratings, so it only lasted two years. Around this same time, "As The World Turns" Head Writer Doug Marland (another Irna Phillips protégé) created one of the most enduring black characters on daytime in lawyer Jessica Griffin. Jessica was played with classy charm by Tamara Tunie from 1987-95 and again from 1999 to 2007. Jessica fell in love with dashing Scotsman Duncan McKechnie (played by Michael Swan) after his wife Shannon died. They faced great opposition from both families, but plodded through the turmoil.

Marland told the story carefully, with just enough naysayers to bring middle America along for the interracial ride. By the time Jessica and Duncan wed, even my fairly close-minded grandmother from Iowa - a fan from the soap's first episode in 1956 - was on board. "They love each other," she said simply.

"I find it sad that [an interracial relationship] is still an issue that has to be addressed, like teenage alcoholism or incest," said Tunie to *Soap Opera Weekly*. "Wouldn't it be ideal to just deal with two people who love each other? When Duncan was involved with Shannon, it was never an issue that he was from Scotland and she was from South Philly."

Shannon returned from the dead, of course, prompting Jessica and Duncan to divorce. But they amicably raised their daughter Bonnie together.

Over the years, every show has tried a similar story, with mixed results. As of 2011, the only African-American characters on daytime were Neil, Lily, Devon, Malcolm and Sophia Winters on "The Young and the Restless," Abe and Lexie Carver on "Days of our Lives," Destiny and Shaun Evans on "One Life To Live," Justin Barber, Marcus Forrester and Dayzee Leigh on "The Bold and the Beautiful," Shawn Butler on "General Hospital," and Brot Monroe, Angie, Jesse and Frankie Hubbard on "All My Children."

DOCTOR, LAWYER, POLICE CHIEF

Soaps haven't done the greatest job integrating black characters and storylines into the action over the years, but it might surprise you to know that while Dr. Martin Luther King was fighting for racial equality in the 1960s, soaps were routinely casting black actors as doctors, lawyers and cops. In fact, some of the biggest African-American actors got their start on soap operas. Here are just a few:

Billy Dee Williams played an Assistant DA on "Another World" from 1964-1966. He left to join sister show "Guiding Light" as Dr. Jim Frazier in 1966.

Cicely Tyson played Jim's wife Martha Frazier on "Guiding Light" in 1966. She was replaced by Ruby Dee in 1967.

James Earl Jones played Dr. Jerry Turner on "As the World Turns." He left to replace Billy Dee Williams as Dr. Jim Frazier on "Guiding Light" in 1967.

Morgan Freeman played Dr. Roy Bingham on "Another World" from 1982-84.

Nia Long played Kat Speakes on "Guiding Light" from 1991 to 1994.

Sharon Leal ("Dreamgirls") played Dahlia Crede on "Guiding Light" from 1996 to 1999.

Taye Diggs played record producer Adrian "Sugar" Hill on "Guiding Light" in 1997.

Rhonda Ross, daughter of Diana Ross and Berry Gordy, played Officer Toni Burrell on "Another World" from 1997 to 1999, earning an Emmy nod in 1998.

Shemar Moore played photographer Malcolm Winters on "The Young and the Restless" from 1997-2005 before hitting it big on "Criminal Minds."

You could certainly make the argument that soaps should have done better with minority storylines, and that they should be working harder to make them work today. But I have to say, they've done a whole lot better with minorities than religion. As I write this, there are no Muslims or Jews on any soap opera. Every soap celebrates Christmas, and every character is Christian, except for "One Life To Live's" Nora Hanen Buchanan, who is half-Jewish. But even she doesn't get a menorah for Hannukah, much less a guest in a yarmulke at any of her weddings.

So yes, race and religion have posed unique challenges for American soap opera storytelling - but not nearly as much as homosexuality...

CHAPTER 8

Gays Of Our Lives

There are even fewer gay characters on soaps than minorities, which is just as surprising. Of *course* homosexuals should busily interact with heterosexuals on soap operas, the same way they do in real life. But no soap has been able to make that work long-term - because gay characters can be a dead end.

The first was a lesbian named Dr. Lynn Carson on "All My Children" in 1983, created once again by pioneer Agnes Nixon. Lynn made vague advances towards Devon Shepherd over a period of months, but the story didn't go anywhere, and Lynn faded away. Fans didn't care, because Lynn was a peripheral character not tied to a major family - the kiss of death on soaps.

The first gay man was more substantive: Hank Elliot on "As The World Turns" in 1988. It had been almost 20 years since the Stonewall Riots in New York City, which marked the beginning of the gay and lesbian movement for equality, and seven years since the first case of AIDS was identified in the U.S. Head writer Doug Marland treaded lightly at first, introducing Hank as a "likeable fashion designer from New York" who had come to rural Oakdale to work with fashionista Barbara Ryan. Hank soon befriended Iva Snyder, who developed a crush on him. Tired of dodging her advances, Hank took Iva out to the Snyder Pond (where all the action happened in the 80s) to tell her the truth.

"This is the talk I've been wanting to have for a while," Hank began. "There is someone in New York, and we've been involved for five years. Iva, I'm gay. I've been involved with another man. We believe in fidelity and mutual support just like anyone else in that kind of relationship. His name is Charles. I love him a lot. I hope you can meet."

The scenes carried over two episodes, with Iva accepting Hank's sexual orientation and encouraging him to come out to his boss, Barbara. Pleased that Iva hadn't pushed him into the Snyder Pond, Hank agreed.

"No more secrets," he vowed.

Fan response was predictably mixed. Since this was before the Internet, it largely amounted to mail sent to the studio. Hank's portrayer, Brian Starcher, told *Soap Opera Digest* in 1988 that many gay men thanked him for being a positive role model, but admitted that not all letters were positive.

"One said, 'It was a real shock when I found out that Hank was queer. I guess it's OK. I still like you anyway. Of course, mama and grandma don't think queers should be on soap operas.'"

Doug Marland crafted Hank carefully, making him a hero when he took a bullet to save a teenaged Paul Stenbeck from his evil father, James. But the story fizzled. Doug told me in 1992 that he considered making Hank HIV positive, but didn't want daytime's only gay character to be sick. He decided instead to give Hank's off-screen partner AIDS, and wrote Hank off in 1989 to be with him.

"I'M BILLY DOUGLAS AND I'M GAY"

The most groundbreaking gay story was told by "One Life To Live" in 1992. Head writer Michael Malone toyed with the idea of making heroine Viki Buchanan's son Joey gay, but ultimately told the story with Joey's high school pal Billy Douglas instead. (*Note: Billy was played by future movie star Ryan Phillippe*).

Billy first confided his orientation to Reverend Andrew Carpenter, who had lost his brother William to AIDS. Andrew counseled the boy to be honest. Billy came out to his father, who spit, "You can't be gay," called him a "pervert," and blamed the Reverend for putting ideas in his son's head. Llanview erupted in scandal, with Andrew accused of molesting Billy and "turning" him gay. The story culminated in Andrew bringing the AIDS quilt to town, and inviting his parishioners to join him as he added a panel for his late brother.

"Love can overcome hatred," urged Andrew.

Billy's father shouted Andrew down, calling him a "gay-loving heretic" in a powerful scene at the church. Billy rose up and announced, "I'm Billy Douglas and I'm gay." Billy's mom embraced him, his dad stormed out, and stunned churchgoers filed out to view the quilt.

The scenes were filmed on location at a church in New Jersey with large panels of the real quilt spread out on the lawn.

"My name is Andrew and I've brought you a brother," he said softly as he added his brother's panel.

His homophobic father Sloan Carpenter, moved by the scene at the church, had an epiphany and joined him. As effective as the story was, though, Billy was also a peripheral character. He soon left town to attend Yale.

HAVING A BALL

ABC expanded on the theme by introducing the annual "Day of Compassion" on all its soaps ("All My Children," "One Life To Live," "General Hospital" and back then, "Port Charles") in 1992. On that day, every show featured an AIDS-related story or scene. "General Hospital" did it best with the Nurses' Ball, part of its HIV/AIDS story involving Robin Scorpio scripted by Head Writer Claire Labine. (Robin contracted HIV from her boyfriend Stone, a former drug user, who died.)

The Nurses' Ball was hosted each year by wacky Lucy Coe and starred all the doctors and nurses at the hospital in funny skits and songs. It wasn't a "gay story" per se, but it did raise AIDS awareness and spotlight gay characters. Actor Lee Mathis, who was HIV positive in real life, was hired to play recurring gay character Jon Hanley after execs saw an ad he placed in the trade magazines asking for work so he could qualify to continue his AFTRA union membership and medical insurance.

"His part was beefed up after his first episode, subsequently adding a specific gay element to the overall AIDS awareness story arc," recalls Scott Barton, who was "General Hospital's" publicist at the time. Even though Mathis's health was failing, "GH" brought him back every year so he could get insurance until his death in 1996.

Despite its huge popularity, ABC dropped the Nurses' Ball in 2001. That was also the last year of the "Day of Compassion."

LESBIANCA

"All My Children" creator Agnes Nixon made headlines again in 2000 when Erica Kane's daughter Bianca came out as a lesbian. That made her the first gay core character on daytime - a milestone.

Wisely, "All My Children" scripted Erica as having trouble with her daughter's revelation, reflecting the feelings of many viewers. Every parent could relate to Erica's concern about her daughter's orientation and its resulting difficulties. The requisite mean girl, Greenlee, cruelly nicknamed her "Lesbianca" and threatened to "out" her, garnering added viewer sympathy for the struggling girl.

Bianca had tentative relationships with Frankie, and then Frankie's twin sister Maggie (don't ask) sparking the cute soap fans' moniker BAM for Bianca And Maggie. Next up was Lena ("Lianca") who provided Bianca's first on-screen kiss. "All My Children" did a good job of cycling women in and out of Bianca's life and giving them interesting story arcs, but there is no romantic jeopardy when there are only two gay girls in town. So Bianca was raped, got pregnant, hid the pregnancy, gave birth, thought the baby (a girl named Miranda) died, and was part of an elaborate baby switch storyline with sister show "One Life To Live" - all the staples needed to keep a character interesting.

Fans embraced her, and daytime's first card-carrying lesbian was a hit. More important, Bianca's portrayer Eden Riegel was a smart, Harvard-educated actress who said all the right things in interviews about gay relationships being the same as straight. Riegel even shared that she happened to have a gay sister, a happy surprise to producers.

The whole story was a stroke of genius. What's more ironic than the most rabidly heterosexual woman in the history of daytime having a gay daughter? Times were changing ("Will and Grace" had debuted in 1998 and was a big hit) and iconic Erica Kane was the perfect character to build the story around. Fans grew to love Bianca and support her relationships. It didn't hurt that ABC got lots of positive press for the story, either.

But by 2007, Bianca's story had lost steam. Riegel elected to leave the show and Bianca moved to Europe. The gay storyline fizzled until a new regime at "All My Children" decided to grab some mainstream press by scripting daytime's first same-sex wedding, and the result was a travesty.

The show didn't do any of the work necessary to build rooting value in a new couple, much less a gay one. Bianca returned from Europe with a sudden lover named Reese (played by "General Hospital" fave Tamara Braun, ex-Carly) and they rushed a story so ridiculous that few bought it. Their hasty wedding in February, 2009 was steeped in cliché, made all the more ridiculous because viewers had seen Reese kiss her future brother-in-law Zach the night before the ceremony.

"You're my miracle," said Reese to Bianca.

"I look into your eyes and I see my soul mate," gushed Bianca. "I promise to be your wife for eternity."

Or until "All My Children" dropped the story, which they quickly did. Never mind that gay marriage wasn't even legal in Pennsylvania, so the entire wedding party trouped to Connecticut in about two scenes. "All My Children" got the press they wanted from publications that don't normally cover soaps, and the requisite awards and recognition from the LGBT community. But by then, the duo had disappeared to France.

Riegel quit "All My Children" in frustration and joined the #1 show "The Young and the Restless." "All My Children" recast Bianca with a less experienced actress, and brought her back with vague, ludicrous explanations of what happened to the missing Reese and their "eternal" marriage.

It was a complete copout.

NUKE and OTALIA

Soaps' first gay male core character came on in 2005, when Lily's son Luke slowly come to the realization that he had feelings for men on "As The World Turns." Luke's biological father Damian rejected his orientation, and tried to convince his son he was straight (gender reassignment camp, anyone?). Eventually, Luke fell for film student Noah, and NUKE was born. They were given good obstacles, including parental disapproval, kidnapping, serial killers and mobsters. "As The World Turns" was on the right track with a well-crafted triangle between Noah, Luke and newcomer Dr. Reid when the show was canceled in 2010. Oh, well.

Sister show "Guiding Light" toyed with making man-crazy Olivia suddenly gay with newcomer Natalia, but the two had barely kissed before the show ended in 2009. Both women were written as bisexual (Natalia was pregnant with Frank's baby when the show got canceled) but "Guiding Light" never fully committed to a lesbian story.

"It wasn't planned to go that way," says a former "Guiding Light" employee. "Crystal Chappell [Olivia] pushed for that story. The progression of that story actually came from the press and from fan response."

One day, Olivia started looking at Natalia a little differently in scenes, and people jumped on it.

"Crystal did her research about a bond that does occur between women of a certain age. She fought for the scenes where Olivia was conflicted: 'Why do I feel this way?' It was not fleshed out as much as she wanted it to be to show the journey this woman was on, but it was played respectfully. I give Crystal so much credit for that. She wanted it to be true and real, and it was."

For as long as it lasted.

As was the case with "All My Children's" Bianca story, "Otalia" garnered widespread fan support, showing that viewers are much more accepting of two women together than two men. I think that's because female soap fans like the fantasy of "having" the hunky man on a soap, and that dream is lost when he is gay. Not so with lesbian characters, who are the object of few straight viewers' affection. They are just pretty girls looking for love.

KISH ME HATE

After NUKE and OTALIA came KISH, the couple who may have put all other soaps off gay couples forever. In 2008, "One Life To Live" created Kyle Lewis (played by Brett Claywell) and Oliver Fish (played by openly gay actor Scott Evans), who came to be known as KISH. Kyle was a doctor and Fish was a cop, the two most important professions on daytime. "One Life To Live" brought them together slowly, built rooting value, and overcame viewer obstacle by having Fish's parents reject him when he came out (poor Fish!). The actors were excellent with the media, teasing the storyline appropriately with the "soap press" while reaching out to mainstream and gay publications as well.

The predictable viewer protests came in to the ABC network, and some in "Middle America" very vocally tuned out. But "One Life To Live" pressed on, eager to tell the story and educate viewers that love comes in all shapes and sexes. However, soon another protest sprung up, accusing "One Life To Live" of being homophobic... *from the gay community.* Their position was, if Kyle and Fish were on two days a week, why weren't they on more? If they kissed once, why not twice? Why couldn't they be the whole show?

"One Life To Live" continued to press on, airing the first gay male love scene on daytime after convincing first the network and then "Standards and Practices" to let them do it. The show offered Evans and Claywell long-term contracts to continue the story, but numerous set sources told me that the actors' demands were too great. One actor asked for "Robin Strasser money," meaning he wanted the same salary as popular Emmy-winner Strasser. (Strasser had joined the show as Dorian Lord in 1979, so that was not a realistic demand.)

"One Life To Live" had no choice but to dump the story, for which they were excoriated by the gay community. "One Life To Live" did not explain why they pulled the plug on the story, nor did they defend the decision. (The networks don't normally comment on contracts, which ties their hands.

They let the actors spin their exits however they choose.)

There were rumblings about backstage trouble with the actors, which were never officially confirmed and frankly aren't germane to the reason they left. But Claywell's reaction when the Daytime Emmy nominations were announced in Spring 2010, and he wasn't nominated after nine months on the soap was telling:

"We tell a story that was groundbreaking and powerful, then lose my job and am overlooked for a nomination. Daytime is such a joke," he tweeted.

Conversely, co-star Evans took the high road, congratulating the "One Life" nominees:

"You are truly remarkable!" he tweeted.

"One Life To Live's" experience with a full-on gay love story became a cautionary tale for all of the other soaps. The unfortunate, harsh truth is that there will be no backlash from middle America OR the gay community if a show never tells a gay love story in the first place.

EXCUSES, EXCUSES

The argument can certainly be made that a good

writer could make any story work on daytime. But let's be honest: Homosexual relationships don't lend themselves to soap opera storytelling.

Bear with me for a minute here…

Let's say a soap brings on a gay character. Who are they going to date? So the soap brings on two gay characters, they date each other, and there's no story. The next problem is the size of the canvas. An hour-long soap has 30+ contract players. There are two or three main families in town, and they all sleep with each other and have kids that grow up to sleep with each other, too. It's not unusual for a character to be with numerous members of the same family.

Look at "The Bold and the Beautiful's" Brooke - she married her "soul mate" Ridge Forrester (and had one kid), his father Eric (two kids), his brother Thorne, and dallied with his son, Thomas. She also had an out of wedlock child with her son-in-law, Deacon. That's three GENERATIONS of Forrester men with one woman, which illustrates the difficulty of integrating a gay character.

It takes a village to sleep with a soap heroine.

And where would soaps be without children that characters forgot they had? No one was more surprised than "All My Children's" Erica when Kendall turned up in 1993 (played by a pre-"Buffy" Sarah Michelle Gellar) as the angry child of a teenage rape Erica had blocked out. "One Life To Live's" Viki had two kids grow to adulthood (Megan and Natalie) before she realized she had given birth to them. Or rather, her alternate personality had given birth to them.

It's easier for men to discover grown offspring they were unaware of, but that still requires sex with a woman. "The Young and the Restless's" Jack was very surprised when Keemo came to town, the child of an affair he had in Viet Nam. "One Life To Live's" Clint fathered Cord and Rex without knowing anything about it. "General Hospital" got a year of story out of Dante arriving in Port Charles to take down famed mobster Sonny Corinthos. But before Sonny could be arrested, he shot Dante in the chest. That prompted Sonny's high school girlfriend Olivia to scream, "You just shot your own son!" Oops.

Of course, a gay character could have a child come out of nowhere too, but it would be much harder to explain.

First of all, gay people don't have accidental pregnancies, which is half of all stories on soap operas. Soap storylines have to go on for years, zig-zagging every which way, depending on who's writing the show and which actors are in favor (i.e. behaving, kissing up to the boss, etc.).A typical story goes like this: Girl sleeps with boyfriend's brother, father, son, best friend; or the boyfriend of her best friend, sister, mother, daughter. Girl gets pregnant, lies about it, changes paternity test, lies some more. Baby gets sick. Blood tests reveal father is not the father. Truth comes out, all hell breaks loose.

It's Soaps 101 as we've discussed, but it can't happen with gay characters, because random encounters don't result in babies. This also explains why characters rarely use birth control, and why condoms are 0% effective on soaps. That said, there are so few homosexuals on television that when a show opens the door, gay people want - and deserve - to barrel through it. But the hate directed at the shows that have made the effort to showcase positive, well-rounded gay characters is counterproductive.

Look at what happened to the hit primetime comedy "Modern Family." The show has two gay dads with a baby enjoying the same screen time and funny lines as all the straight people on the show. Yet there was a backlash the show's first year *from the gay community* that the gay dads didn't kiss - never mind that no one kisses on that show.

"I never understood why people put their focus on 'Modern Family,' a show that introduced a loving, grounded gay couple on television who adopted a baby, and accused it of being homophobic," mused Cam's portrayer, Eric Stonestreet, to the *New York Times* in January 2010.

Amen, brotha.

SEARCH FOR TOMORROW

Currently, there are two gay characters on soaps: "All My Children's" recast Bianca, and "Young and Restless" lawyer Rafe, who is not a contract player. As I write this, "Days of our Lives" is said to be embarking on the tale of Sami's son Will coming out and dating the son of a local scion. The next should be on "The Bold and the Beautiful," because it is not logical that the show is set in the LA fashion industry and doesn't have one gay person working in any of its fashion houses.

In my opinion, the best way to tell a gay story would be to have a character that fans already know come out, like Bianca did. Tell the story slowly, show the character's struggle, and make them sympathetic. Take the audience on their "journey." (I hate that word, but it applies here.) Use the show's valuable connection to viewers to broaden their horizons.

Like it or not, a certain segment of soap fans do not want to watch two people of the same sex falling in love, and they will be very vocal communicating that to the network. So the crucial element in a successful gay love story has to be the support of the gay community. Rather than criticizing a story for being told too slowly or lacking in love scenes, be positive about it. Write a letter to the network supporting the character(s) and saying you want to see more of them. Post positive comments on soap web sites and Facebook pages, particularly the ones run by the networks.

And, most of all - *be patient.* Despite all the fantastic male nudes that decorate it, even Rome wasn't built in a day.

The very first show I watched with my mom was "General Hospital." The characters and intrigue are what hooked me. As a teenager, I thought it was fascinating that doctors and nurses had real lives too, and that drama occurred in the work place. "GH" had stories that many people identified with, but never really discussed or acted on in their own lives.

We also watched "The Young and The Restless" together later on. I was fascinated by Liz Foster, the maid who never cleaned. My favorite character was Ashley. I thought it was cool that a young woman had a powerful job and no one took her seriously — partly because she was an Abbott but mostly because she was pretty.

My mom and sister watched "Days" too but I never got into that one. I remember they watched Bo and Hope's wedding together and threw rice at the TV. I thought that was hysterical. I was always drawn to the stories of powerful women and I loved watching them win. Just because soaps have been on the air for a long time doesn't mean they don't still offer interesting, exciting television. I love these shows for many reasons, but mostly because I feel like I know these people. I work from home, and I am even getting my husband hooked.

Paying it forward, like my mom did.

- **Cynthia from West Virginia**

CHAPTER 9

Soaps: The First Social Network

Interracial romance, homosexuality, divorce, alcoholism, mental illness, unwanted pregnancy, abortion, impotence, addiction, incest, Down Syndrome, suicide, anorexia, HIV/AIDS, rape, adultery... you name it, Daytime has dealt with it.

NO other form of entertainment has so effectively addressed social issues.

Naturally, it was Irna Phillips who perfected the art of weaving difficult topics into her storytelling. As outlined in Chapter One, she got the wartime ball rolling on radio by scripting Reverend Ruthledge's daughter Mary befriending a Jewish girl, and a veteran discussing his disability during World War II. Phillips was always looking for ways to incorporate important issues into her ongoing drama.

"Irna did a show once in which a young woman had Lupus," Agnes Nixon recalled to the Museum of Broadcasting. "At one point, the characters were talking about this girl when she wasn't there, because Irna thought it was important that the girl not hear them say, 'Oh, that's incurable.' But all the people who had Lupus, whose doctors told them it was curable, were listening. The show was inundated with calls. It really made Irna sit up and take notice. She said, 'Never try to do a disease that's incurable.' I picked uterine cancer because that is 100% curable if caught in time."

Indeed, Nixon scripted "Guiding Light's" heroine Bert Bauer getting a Pap Smear way back in 1962 that showed Bert was in the early stages of uterine cancer. The honchos at P&G weren't too keen on "Guiding Light's" matriarch getting a Pap Smear (hey, at least it was off-camera), but Nixon fought and won the battle to educate viewers. Bert's cancer played out in real time, emphasizing cancer prevention, and fans responded positively.

Educating fans about cancer has been a major theme with daytime's large female audience, particularly breast cancer. "One Life To Live's" Viki and "Guiding Light's" Lillian both suffered long, ultimately triumphant bouts with the disease, but it was the wrenching journey of "General Hospital's" Monica Quartermaine in 1994-95 that is most remembered.

"You've never looked more beautiful to me," insisted her husband, Alan, after Monica had a mastectomy.

"Liar!" she responded, opening her robe (with her back to the camera, duh) to reveal her scar. "Do you honestly think this is sexy? Try making love to THIS!"

"I miss you, Monica. Not your breast," said Alan softly.

It took Monica a long time to feel "whole" again, and "General Hospital" played every beat of her struggle with cancer treatment centers, support groups, and Monica turning to young Dr. Pierce Dorman to try and feel sexy again.

Monica later tied Pierce up in an effort to get him to confess to dealing drugs, but that was a different story.

IT'S COMPLICATED

One of the most difficult scenes that ever aired on "Guiding Light" involved the never-before-tackled topic of marital rape.

They told the story with journalist Holly Norris and her villainous husband Roger Thorpe in 1979. The two had been having problems for a while. When she tried to leave, he caught her writing him a "Dear Roger" letter and stopped her dead in her tracks.

Roger (advancing): "We could have a swell time if you'd forget your petty resentments."

Holly: "Don't touch me."

Roger badgered Holly about her feelings for Ed Bauer, threw her suitcase across the room, and then reminded her of her… marital obligations.

Roger: "I am your husband. I have certain rights here."

Holly: "No! Leave me alone!"

Roger threw Holly on the bed and we heard screams.

The action picked up after the rape. Roger took a drink as Holly touched her torn clothes and then escaped to find Ed.

Ed's brother Mike Bauer helped Holly prosecute Roger for marital rape. When it looked like Roger's hot new attorney Ross Marler was going to get him acquitted, Holly caught Roger attacking Ed and pumped three bullets into him. That led right into another social issue story - women in prison - after Holly was stabbed by a jealous female inmate.

Most soap heroines have done time in prison, but none so fashionably as "All My Children's" Erica Kane. Erica went to federal prison for insider trading sporting the only custom-made orange jumpsuit in history, complete with a cinched waist and cuffs.

Erica crusaded for a jobs program while behind bars to help the women find employment upon their release and was soon released for good behavior.

RISKY BUSINESS

"Good behavior," is relative on soaps. One of the biggest struggles for writers has been the issue of safe sex. Of course every character should be practicing birth control and using condoms, but, as outlined in the previous chapter, that would eliminate all the unwanted pregnancies and out-of-wedlock children that keep stories spinning.

"General Hospital" took a big risk in 1994-95 with the story of former drug user Stone Cates having unprotected sex with his angelic girlfriend Robin Scorpio. Later, Stone discovered he was HIV Positive and had given Robin the virus. It was a brave story to tell, because Robin was a legacy character (daughter of infamous WSB agents Robert and Anna Scorpio) and fans had watched her and her portrayer, Kimberly McCullough literally grow up on the show.

Not surprisingly, some viewers didn't like it.

"Daytime is reflective of where the world is," defended Head Writer Claire Labine to *Soap Opera Digest* in 1997. "It's the escapist fantasy of the day. In different times, there were different idioms that worked. When Luke and Laura were running around saving the world from the Cassadines, that was the standard soap paradigm for that time and place. Now, the shows have moved on. That doesn't make them better or worse than before. They're just different."

What's different today is that characters rarely discuss birth control and men never use condoms. It's like they went through the "phase" of being responsible and now have to get back to the business of impregnating the wrong people. The only "bad" thing that ever comes out of unprotected sex on soaps today is unwanted pregnancy. Typically, the girl is not happy to learn she is pregnant, considers aborting the baby (the shows keep lots of handy pamphlets around for the girl to study, as well as for her husband/boyfriend to find) and then she accepts her condition. Curiously, with all this unsafe sex, no one has gotten a disease since Robin contracted HIV in 1995.

The only other case of a sexually transmitted disease that I can recall was Nikki contracting VD from Paul on "The Young and the Restless" in the late 1970s. It was a brief story blip that was never mentioned again - including 25 years later, when Nikki and Paul reunited, and even got engaged for a while. They had a series of romantic conversations, none of which included their former brush with venereal disease. I get why the show didn't want to walk down that particular memory lane but it sure would have been a great place for product placement.

"Did you take your Valtrex today, honey?"

Perhaps Nikki didn't dwell on it because she started life in Genoa City having murdered her own father to stop him from raping her. Problems are relative on daytime. Bill Bell told other social issue stories, too, but as Christopher Schemering points out in the *Soap Opera Encyclopedia*, he was a little clumsy about it when he started.

"Did you know one out of ten girls is a mother before she is 18?" asked one character.

"Wow, that's a mind blower. What can we do?" responded another.

Bell had better luck when Snapper and Casey Reed demonstrated the Heimlich maneuver for viewers with the appropriately grope-y sexual overtones. He even took a page from his old boss Irna Phillips and scripted a scene in 1996 where Nikki talked to her young daughter Victoria about the importance of Pap tests.

PERSONALITY PLUS

Like Nikki Newman, "One Life To Live's" Victoria

Lord was sexually assaulted by her father, Victor Lord. But rather than hit him on the head with a lamp like Nikki did, Viki developed alternate personalities to deal with the trauma. That allowed Agnes Nixon to educate viewers about Disassociative Identity Disorder while also gaining the storyline opportunity to have Viki commit crimes without having to go to jail. Viki's alternate personalities did all the dirty work: Tori killed Victor Lord and set fire to the family mansion Llanfair; Jean held Dorian prisoner in a secret room at Llanfair; Niki killed Johnny Dee and pushed Viki's husband Ben out a window.

Ben's death worked out well for Viki, though, because although she missed him, she needed a heart transplant and Ben turned out to be a perfect match. That story then segued into a peppy, educational tale about women and heart disease.

DON'T MANIC

Most of soaps' social issue stories just involve actors playing roles, but Maurice Benard's experience as "General Hospital's" Sonny Corinthos hit way too close to home.

Benard was diagnosed as manic depressive in his 20s and was prescribed Lithium. He moved to New York from California, landed a role on "All My Children" in 1987, and managed fine during his three-year run as Nico Kelly. The actor then moved to LA, eventually joining "General Hospital" as moody mobster Sonny Corinthos in 1993. The show elected to make ongoing issues with depression part of Sonny's story (long before anyone had ever heard of 1999's Tony Soprano, mind you), which prompted Benard to go off his medication in an effort to deliver a more "real" performance. His work was raw and powerful, but it led to a breakdown for the actor.

"It was probably about a week's time that I saw the transformation," Benard's wife Paula told Oprah Winfrey in 2004. "It wasn't just one moment or one day that it happened. Literally, you see someone becoming a totally different person.""That's the problem with this disease," added Benard. "You always deny. 'I'm fine, I'm fine, I'm fine.' Until you get to that point. And unfortunately, at the end of the story, I got to that point."Benard had a breakdown. With support from Paula and his "GH" family, Benard battled back and is now medication compliant.

"I flirt with not taking it, but I'm not stupid. Every time I've gone off the medication, I've had a breakdown."

He won the Emmy for Outstanding Lead Actor in 2003.

In the last few years, Benard has worked with Mental Health America as the spokesperson for Bipolar Disorder, doing numerous interviews about the illness, and becoming a role model for people with similar afflictions.

"Pretty much everywhere I go, people come up to me and say, 'Thank you for helping me,'" he told Oprah. "It's great to educate people on what this disease does and what it is."

A BOLD STORY

It's harder for "The Bold and the Beautiful" to tell social issue stories, because the show airs in over 100 countries. How do you dub "A black child deserves two black parents!" into 100 languages, including countries in Africa? Is there a word for Lithium in Swahili?

But the show found a way in 2010 when matriarch Stephanie Forrester was diagnosed with cancer and wanted to give her life meaning outside of the family she raised. The show crafted a moving story about Stephanie reaching out to the homeless, which resulted in visits to real LA-area homeless shelters, and appearances by real homeless people.

"We had an overwhelming response to our homeless story on a national and local level," reports "B&B" rep Eva Demirjian. "LA's local Union Rescue Mission received 800 emails on the first day of the Public Service Announcement, alone."

Strangely, soaps haven't told too many stories about infertility, even though it is a big topic for real women in their 30s and 40s. We were much more likely to see "GL's" Reva getting pregnant in her fifties after having cancer than we were to see a conversation between Reva and her much younger husband Jeffrey about whether or not she could give him children. Erica Kane is a grandmother many times over, yet the only conversation she had with the 20-years younger Ryan on "All My Children" when they were dating was "What will Kendall think?"

Ditto for "One Life To Live's" hilarious Dorian and David who had a quickie wedding before he headed off to star in his own life story.

"I dream of doing something really important for this country," he explained. "Being famous."

I get that soaps are a women's medium and that we are to be celebrated on every episode. Women aging out of their childbearing years yet still dating younger men does feel like an area fraught with possibility.

I mean, even Irna Phillips adopted kids as a single mother in her 40s.

My personal favorite line about a late-in-life pregnancy came from "Dynasty's" Alexis to Krystal after Krystal bragged that she had been "blessed" with Blake Carrington's baby.

"Oh please, Krystal," snarked Alexis. "Even worms procreate."

NO SMOKING

I was surprised to find in James Thurber's 1948 writings about soap operas in *The New Yorker* that P&G

used smoking on its soaps to indicate villainy in a character. Tobacco companies were a huge advertiser back then – Phillip Morris sponsored the hottest TV show in the fifties, "I Love Lucy" – so that was really cutting off their (cancerous) nose to spite their face.

"In daytime radio," wrote Thurber, "the cigarette has come to be a sign of evil that ranks with the mark of the cloven hoof, the scarlet letter, and the brand of the fleur-de-lis. The married woman who smokes a cigarette proclaims herself a bad wife or an unnatural mother or an adventuress. The male cigarette smoker is either a gangster or a cold, calculating white-collar criminal. A man who called on the hero of 'Young Doctor Malone' brought him some excellent pipe tobacco and announced that he himself would smoke a fine cigar. As if to take the edge off this suggestion of wanton sensual abandon, a good woman hastily said to the caller, 'Don't you want a nice, cold glass of ice water?' 'Splendid!' cried the gentleman... and the virtue of the household was reestablished."

How many smoking-related deaths were prevented because P&G was 20 years ahead of the U.S. Surgeon General (which didn't declare smoking hazardous until 1964) in making cigarettes not cool? No other entertainment medium has survived and thrived for 81 years, *or* saved as many lives. More than any other art form, soaps depict what is going on at the time - social, racially, economically, and politically - and they do it fearlessly, with great care and humor.

Backstage, however, is another story...

CHAPTER 10
It's Not Always T.I.I.C.*

(*The Idiots In Charge)

Actors are a talented, good-looking bunch, but WOW can they be their own worst enemies. The biggest backstage problem on soaps has been drugs and alcohol. Not only does an actor's destructive behavior hurt him, it hurts his co-stars and the entire production. And it costs money soaps cannot afford.

ALL MY DRUG DENS

Remember Michael Nader? He was the dreamy actor who played Dex Dexter on "Dynasty" in the 1980s, and then joined "All My Children" as Dimitri Marick in 1991.

Nader was cruising along nicely as a popular love interest for Susan Lucci's Erica. Dimitri had his own estate (Wildwind), with a living room and a bedroom set. He had a stable for his "horses," which was really just for people to have sex in. He had a Pulitzer prize-winning brother, Edmund Grey, a hot sister-in-law Dr. Maria Grey (played by "CSI: Miami's" Eva LaRue), and a handsome son, Anton. He married Erica Kane in a lavish, expensive ceremony, then had steamy sex with his brother Edmund's wife, Maria and was thought to have fathered her baby. Maria's baby was delivered by Erica in a storm, of course. He was even on the board at Pine Valley Hospital.

Dimitri had everything a dashing soap hero could want, so what went wrong?

Michael Nader got arrested.

In August of 1997, Nader was arrested for drunk driving with his 13 year-old daughter in the car. He pleaded guilty to driving while intoxicated and was ordered to spend 20 days in rehab. Numerous sources told me at the time that ABC paid for Nader's rehab. Upon completion, he was welcomed back to the show and resumed working.

Nader was arrested again in 2001 in an illegal Manhattan social club and charged with possession of cocaine and attempting to sell cocaine. The charges were downgraded to misdemeanor possession, and Nader was ordered by the court to undergo drug rehabilitation. This time, however, ABC did not pay for Nader's rehab. It was co-star Mark Consuelos (ex-Mateo) who helped him.

"Mark stood by my side," Nader told *Soap Opera Digest* in 2003. "He was very instrumental. I had to wait, like, seven days, for Betty Ford. He helped me, and within three days I got into Hazelden. At that stage I was pretty shattered, and Mark picked up the ball and helped me. It was a financial concern I could not meet."

The first time Nader faced trouble, "All My Children" was able to move Dimitri to the backburner, so that fans didn't notice his absence while Nader got clean. The second time, though, Dimitri was too heavy in story, so they had to do an emergency recast with former "Guiding Light" star Anthony Addabbo (ex-Jim Lemay). One day, fans just heard *"The role of Dimitri Marick is now being played by Anthony Addabbo"* and that was it.

Obviously, this was a difficult time for Nader, but imagine the toll it took on the show and his co-stars. What was going on before he got busted? Was he showing up on time? Did he know his lines? How much did it cost to move scenes around on the days he was in jail, rehab, or unable to work? How did his troubles impact his co-star Susan Lucci (Erica)? I don't think it's a coincidence that Erica and Dimitri broke up soon after Nader's first arrest in 1997 and the show brought on soap vet Vincent Irizarry as Lucci's new love interest, David Hayward.

Life went on in Pine Valley. Nader was not rehired after the second incident. Addabbo played the role for three months until Dimitri could be sent to Europe.

Dimitri has never been seen or heard from since.

AS THE WORLD BACKSTAGE TURNS

The sudden recasting of a character usually indicates

backstage trouble or illness.

The worst example of both was Michael David Morrison, who played Caleb Snyder on "As The World Turns" from 1988 to 1993. He was found dead of a drug overdose in a bed not his own. The coroner's report said, "acute intoxication caused by the combination of ethanol, cocaine and opiates." Out of deference to his wife and young son, the soap magazines did not report details. Clearly, this was before the Internet.

Six years later, another "As The World Turns" star, Nathaniel Marston, got arrested for "criminal mischief" while playing Eddie Silva. Seems an ATM ate his bank card one night and he got so angry he tried to rip the machine out of the wall. Taping had to be frantically re-jiggered the next morning because Marston was in jail when he was supposed to be at work.

The powers-that-be were not amused. Marston was written off in 2000, when Eddie inherited $25 million and left town with his new wife, Georgia. The talented actor was popular with fans, though, and seemed to have a handle on his troubles. So "One Life To Live" took a chance on him and hired him as Al Holden the next year. Al was killed off in a convoluted 2003 tale in which his spirit entered the body of Dr. Michael McBain. (The soap needed a well-liked brother for moody John McBain.)

But Marston was soon in trouble again. He badly injured his foot jumping from a roof, necessitating surgery and a hastily written story explaining why Michael was on crutches. He was notoriously late for work, to the point where he had four alarm clocks, as well as co-stars calling him to wake him up. He eventually hired someone to come to his apartment every morning to make sure he was awake.

Marston was arrested again in 2007 for assaulting three people, including a police officer, resulting in his own hospitalization at Bellevue Hospital. He was charged with felony assault, reckless endangerment and criminal possession of a weapon. That was too much for the soap. They replaced Marston and eventually wrote the character off in 2009.

"The role of Michael McBain is now being played by Chris Stack."

For every story like these, there are dozens more that fans don't hear about. Here's how it usually goes: The producer, directors and/or co-stars notice something is wrong with an actor and go to the boss. The Executive Producer then has to go to the legal department for help dealing with the actor. A meeting is held with the actor, asking them to please not drink at work (!) or whatever the issue is. That is considered a warning. If it continues, sterner measures are taken that can lead to firing.

Often, fans notice when something is not right with an actor. He or she has gained or lost a lot of weight, the eyes are glassy, or they are slurring their words. If the actor refuses to shape up, the show generally moves the actor to the backburner and gets rid of them. In extreme cases, they recast with the explanation that they are "taking the character in a different direction."

"Soaps are a place where if there is smoke, there's probably fire," laughs former "Guiding Light" Costume Designer Shawn Dudley. "They used to let me know when someone's contract was ending, because they didn't want me to go out and spend money on clothes for someone who was leaving. I always kept my mouth shut. But then the rumors would start and the smoke would start to rise, and I would watch it spiral until the show had to confirm the actor's exit."

It's harder to protect actors who ruin their faces with plastic surgery. Soaps are on tape, which is a much less forgiving format than film. Soaps also depend heavily on the close-up, which is a horror show with a bad face job. Again, execs tend to move these people to the backburner, and then drop them to recurring. Fans demand, "Where's so-and-so?" Um, have you seen her lately? That actress can't play a story if her face doesn't move.

SEX, LIES ON VIDEOTAPE

Sex is another problem for execs. Specifically, actors hooking up.

"The lack of sunlight contributes to that, too," quips Hunt Block.

It's fantastic when it works out – "All My Children's" Kelly Ripa and Mark Consuelos (Hayley and Mateo), "One Life To Live's" James and Kassie DePaiva (Max and Blair), "As The World Turns'" Scott DeFreitas and Maura West (Andy and Carly), etc. - but a nightmare when it doesn't. You have no idea how many soap couples have broken up onscreen because their portrayers took it too far off-screen.

One überpopular duo were rumored to have hooked up a few times during their early days of working together, but two decades later, he was happily married and the bloom was definitely off the rose. The TV wife was so jealous of the attention her TV husband and his new, younger co-star were getting that she spread a false rumor that they were having an affair.

Another duo's relationship was the worst-kept secret on this west-coast set. Despite the fact that she was seriously dating another soap star and he was married, these two - who were also paired on screen - carried on at work like they were single and free to mingle, much to the discomfort of the other actors, who could hear them in their dressing room.

Aside from the obvious awkwardness of listening to co-stars have sex; most affairs inevitably go horribly wrong. That's when one or both of the sex-havers has been known to go to the boss and ask out of the onscreen relationship. It takes months to change a story, and it is murder to do it when you have a popular couple.

Backstage sex is especially hard if the sex-havers are married to other people. Sometimes, co-stars are friends with the cheater's spouse, and feel guilty watching it go on. Some have been known to confront the actor, or even tell the cuckolded spouse. More uneasiness.

How about actors who sexually harass their partner? It's the show's obligation to protect its actresses. If they can't stop it, they have to break up the couple or even fire the actor. But you'll never hear them explain it as, "We had to fire so-and-so because he refused to stop tonguing his co-star during their love scenes."

Or actors who make passes at young day players? There's a famous story about a big-named actor who used to wear a bathrobe around the studio and flash his junk to the extras. Often, they were scared to complain for fear of losing their job. To that show's credit, the actor eventually lost HIS job.

Of course some extras are very willing to fool around with the star of the show. One time, the wife of a popular actor suspected he was playing hide-the-script with various day players and secretly placed a nanny-cam in his dressing room.

He was, and she caught him. As tough as that was on the couple, it was beyond uncomfortable for the entire cast and crew, which knew all about it.

And did you hear the one about the actor who beat up his girlfriend and got served with a restraining order at work? He refused to come out of his dressing room, so an exec had to sign for the order. That went over well.

The actor was gone within six months.

PRETTY IS AS PRETTY DOES

Some reasons for ousting an actor aren't nearly as sinister. Have you ever noticed when an actress's hair changes in the middle of a "soap day"? On Tuesday she has long brown hair, and on Wednesday she has short blonde hair, yet the action picks up in the middle of the scene? This is because the actress did not get the show's approval to change her look. Most actors make it easy on themselves by getting their hair cut and colored at the studio. It's easy to throw a line into a script ("Nice hair!") on a new soap day, but much harder in the middle.

I was at "General Hospital" the day one of their biggest actresses came in with a shocking shorter haircut. They had to rearrange the entire day (inconveniencing every other actor and costing who knows how much money) to add hair extensions to her head before they could film that day's scenes. No matter how good the writers are, they can't explain how someone's hair got six inches shorter between commercials.

Finally, you have the actors who are just your standard issue pain-in- the-ass. They refuse to tape scenes because "my character would never do that," forgetting that the writers decide what their characters will and will not do. One famous villain was so guilty of this that all seven directors banded together and went to the Executive Producer, asking that the show get rid of him. They did.

"I'll never understand actors who don't want to play the bad things their characters are supposed to do," muses Thorsten Kaye, who played Patrick Thornhart on "One Life To Live" and Zach Slater on "All My Children." Kaye cites an actor on "All My Children" who would routinely take out any bad or angry things scripted for his character.

"He would say, 'My character wouldn't do that,' and I would say, 'Yeah, he would. It says it right here on page 4.' Actors take the bite out of the scenes when they do that. There's no redemption if you never do anything bad. Fans want to see characters redeemed."

Kaye agrees that some actors identify too closely with their characters, and consequently don't want to play "bad" for fear of fans turning on them. He feels the opposite, recalling when Zach shot Josh Madden after Josh took Reese hostage at the casino in 2009.

"I wanted to shoot Colin [Egglesfield, who played Josh] right in the face. I said, 'Let me shoot him in cold blood and then deal with it after.' They said no."

Which Kaye thought was a mistake.

"For us to breathe life into these characters, we need to show that there is good and bad in everybody. We need to make them three-dimensional. It's not wrong for an actor to question something in a script, saying, 'I can't understand this.' But it's wrong to say, 'I'm not going to play this.' That's our job."

Three-time Emmy winner Peter Bergman (Jack, "The Young and the Restless") agrees. I can't tell you how many times I have sat in his CBS dressing room and talked about how he can't wait to get his scripts.

"I don't want to write for Jack," he says. "I want to play Jack."

"General Hospital's" Tony Geary also agrees. But he told *TV Guide's* Michael Logan in March 2011 that an exec actually came to him this spring to ask if it would be okay if Luke ran down his own grandson, Jake, while driving under the influence.

"I thought it was odd that he asked for my OK," Geary told Logan. "Even [executive producer] Jill Phelps said, 'You don't have to do this,' which I couldn't understand at all."

Geary posited that perhaps his former co-star Sarah Brown's unhappiness with her character Claudia's child-killing had something to do with "GH's" reticence.

"They had some trouble with Sarah Brown before she left the show," revealed Geary. "Her character was going to be responsible for a child's death and she went completely nuts about it saying, 'You're ruining the image and I won't do it,' and blah, blah, blah. That never made any sense to me. So maybe they were a little sensitive after that."

Thorsten Kaye, Peter Bergman and Tony Geary are three of the most respected leading men in the business, routinely up for Emmys every year. It would behoove some of these less experienced yahoos to take a page from their books and play the drama as written - even if means they have to get a little (fake) blood on their hands.

NAILED IT

Actors don't just have flare-ups about storylines. Over the years, they have complained about everything from the kind of shoes their character is wearing to the color of their nail polish.

I'm not kidding. One diva refused to work one day until her female scene partner changed her nail polish, saying her character would never wear the same nail color as anyone else in town. Another diva wouldn't play a scene until the show bought her character a new coat, saying her character would never wear last season's clothes.

One big fan favorite is referred to as "The Beast" backstage because she likes picking fights and causing trouble. Her problems with wardrobe are legendary. Once, she refused to wear the dress they gave her for that day's scenes because she hadn't shaved her legs.

"Go shave your legs in the bathroom," begged the wardrobe person. "Better yet, you're making $6,000 a show - go get your legs waxed."

Another time, she refused to wear a low-cut top because she wanted her character taken seriously. They put her in a crisp blouse, and she complained to the executive producer that she wasn't being dressed sexy enough.

"She's such an amazing actress, but no one wants to work with her," sighs the wardrobe head.

The actors may not see these kinds if incidents as bad behavior, but the shows do - because it takes up time they don't have.

HAVE SOME COKE AND A SMILE

All of these backstage problems pull focus away from the work, upset the cast and crew, and cost valuable time and money. They also anger the networks. Yet, fans rarely hear any of these stories. That's because Daytime protects its own, which really sets it apart from the rest of the entertainment industry.

"You're right," affirms former "General Hospital" publicist Scott Barton. "No other area of entertainment protects their own with such conviction. In my experience working on 'GH,' the cast and crew spent more time together than with their families. We *were* a family. We laughed, cried, screamed, dished and hugged each other every single day - as you know! No one gets by without carrying their load, but no one carries it alone either. There are legal and HR issues when someone has problems that are dealt with privately. But aside from the corporate crap that must be addressed, the daytime realm is a clan - and when the going gets tough, you circle 'round, defend and protect your own. I never felt safer or more cared for than when I was in Port Charles."

That's one of the biggest attractions of working on a soap opera, the feeling of family. Dysfunctional sometimes? Yes. But still a family.

Personally, I don't think fans want to know if their favorite actor is doing drugs or cheating on their spouse or refusing to kiss their co-star. These are people in your living room every day. You want to think they are worthy of your time and attention - and honestly, most of them are.

I give execs a lot of credit for taking the rap for their troubled actors. They take the notion that soaps are a family to the nth degree. The shows never acknowledge when an actor has a drug or alcohol problem. Even when fans are blasting them for getting rid of a fave, the bosses don't say a word. They just eat the bad press. The same goes for fellow actors - most will only discuss a troubled co-star off the record.

I have always thought the shows should be more honest, but they prefer to take the heat than defuse viewer wrath. They may be right. For all the bitching and moaning from fans when changes are made, they'd probably be even more unhappy to learn that their favorite actor is a jerk. On soaps, the actor is protected to the end.

And for that, soaps are to be commended - because no other area of the entertainment industry does that.

Just ask Charlie Sheen.

CHAPTER 11

But Sometimes It Is
T.I.I.C.* Fault
*The Idiots In Charge

While actors mess up in selfish and substance abuse-y ways, executives make mistakes that are far more damaging. I'll never understand how a network could put someone in charge of their daytime lineup who doesn't understand why people watch soap operas. The whole point of a soap is to hook people with vibrant stories and characters, and get them to tune in every day. It's a simple, basic format, perfected by Irna Phillips with the now-standard cliffhanger.

So how is it possible that network execs have repeatedly disrupted their daily storytelling with preemptions that literally drove millions of eyeballs away?

I AM NOT A CROOK - BUT I WILL PREEMPT YOUR SOAPS!

The first chink in soap opera's once-strong armor occurred with the Senate Watergate Hearings in the summer of 1973. All three major networks (there was no CNN at the time) preempted their daytime lineups beginning on May 17, 1973 to air testimony relating to whether President Richard Nixon, his Attorney General John Mitchell, or others in the executive office knew anything about a break-in at the Democratic National Committee offices in the Watergate building. White House aide John Dean soon testified that Nixon knew of the plan, as well as the resulting elaborate cover-up, and things spiraled down for Nixon as the summer progressed.

Yes, it was important national news, and yes it brought down a President. But it was not necessary for every network to air the same exact coverage every day in place of what was then their 16 soap operas. The networks eventually realized that, and started rotating coverage to every third day. Meanwhile, PBS began airing a taped version of that day's testimony every night. The hearings concluded on August 7, 1973, at which point regularly programming thankfully was restored.

When the Watergate Hearings resumed on September 24, 1973, public interest was not as strong and the networks had learned what happens when you interrupt the flow of your "stories." They did not preempt like that again, but the damage had been done.

The number one soap "As The World Turns" had an 11.1 Nielsen rating during the 1971-72 season going in to the Watergate Hearings. Richard Nixon resigned the Presidency on August 8, 1974. After the dust settled, "As The World Turns" was still number one in 1975, but with a 9.4. Since one ratings point equaled 874,000 viewing homes back then, that meant 1.5 million fewer people were now watching the top soap.

Worse, "Return To Peyton Place" and "How To Survive a Marriage" did not survive the 1974 season. Daytime went from 16 to 14 soaps on the air.

IF IT DOESN'T FIT, YOU MUST ACQUIT - AND PRE-EMPT AGAIN.

Stunningly, network execs made the exact same mistake 20 years later, with the trial of former football star O.J. Simpson. He was tried in Los Angeles criminal court for the June, 1994 deaths of his ex-wife Nicole Brown Simpson and her friend Ronald Goldman. The trial ran from January to October in 1995, doing irreparable damage to the soap line-ups, as networks routinely preempted willy-nilly during the entire ten-month trial.

Here is a list of ratings as reported by Nielsen Media Research for the 1993-94 season (left) compared to the 1996-97 season when the trial was over (right):

The Young and the Restless	8.6 /7.1
All My Children	6.6/4.7
General Hospital	6.2/4.8
The Bold and the Beautiful	6.1/5.0
As the World Turns	5.8/4.4
One Life to Live	5.6/4.0
Days of our Lives	5.6/5.8

Guiding Light	**5.4/4.0**
Another World	**3.5/3.1**
Loving	**2.7/1.8**

"One thing's for sure, O.J. Simpson is a murderer," pronounced Jon Mandel, a senior VP at Grey Advertising, to Ad Age Magazine in 1995. "He killed daytime TV."

All three networks initially preempted their soaps, not thinking ahead about what that would do to regular television viewing patterns. Fans, media, and the shows themselves never knew from day to day if their soap would be on. Decisions to preempt were minute to minute, and varied in every market across the country.

And then there were the days when the trial would recess or adjourn early, and the soaps would just pick up in the middle.

"I remember it being total hell in my office," recalls Scott Barton, who was the publicist of "General Hospital" at the time. "Various media outlets were contacting me about show episodes being pre-empted and rerun all through the interminable OJ trial. So many of my PR efforts to highlight specific storylines and actors got dumped by shows like "GMA," "Extra" and "ET" because some OJ flare up occurred that bumped my time-specific stories."

After a few months, execs realized their daytime lineups were hemorrhaging, and tried to resume soap business as usual. But it was too late. The continuing drama of O.J. Simpson, Kato Kaelin, the Brown family and the Goldman family was airing on Court TV, CNN and E! by this point, and fans hadn't seen Erica Kane or Victor Newman for months - so they turned to cable to "stay tuned."

ABC, NBC and CBS execs had done the worst possible thing: They had hooked rabid soap fans on the O.J. Simpson trial by preempting their regular soaps, and then sent them to cable to see how it ended.

"Wally Kurth (who played Ned) and I watched the OJ verdict in my office" sighs Barton. "Once we regained our ability to speak following that completely ludicrous 'Not guilty' decision, I remember saying to him, 'Well, I hope things get back to normal quickly... whatever normal is now.'"

There was no more "normal." Ad Age estimated that Court TV, CNN and E! had "cannibalized about 20% of the

Big 3's daytime TV rating points." If you look at the previous page's ratings numbers, that's about right.

And most of those viewers never returned.

ENTER STAGE LEFT: THE INTERNET

You can't blame the O.J. trial solely for the drop-off in viewers around this time. Ironically, it was soap fans trying to keep up with their shows on the Internet that struck the next blow.

Because the O.J. preemptions were day-to-day and varied throughout the country, soap opera fan sites started cropping up on the Internet. A fan would watch "All My Children" on the East Coast, for example, and then post a complete synopsis of that day's events for the West Coast, where preemptions were much more frequent because of the local angle of the trial. Some shows got out of sequence, so they aired a day ahead in parts of the country. Fans helpfully posted the complete goings-on for their counterparts in areas saddled with continued O.J. coverage.

More and more fans started logging in for "spoilers" of shows that hadn't aired yet, and talking to each other on websites. Message boards exploded, with each thread about a character or story logging thousands of comments.

This should have been a positive development, but the networks did not respond well to this. Rather than create their own sites, with better spoilers and exclusive photos to match, they tried to stop the juggernaut of information getting out. They halted studio tours to fans to insure no one posted the inside info before they wanted it out, and made actors and employees sign agreements not to disclose upcoming story. The soap magazines were ordered not to give any spoilers away on their Internet sites, effectively killing all the live chats, because all fans wanted to know was "Is so-and-so going to get pregnant/get married/die?" and the editors couldn't tell them. Meanwhile, viewers could go to any number of fan sites and get the information. So, all the new, excited, coveted YOUNG soap eyeballs were going to bootleg fan sites instead of to the networks' own sites, or even the sanctioned sites of the soap magazines.

Once again, the execs had driven what should have been their own traffic somewhere else.

YOUTH IS WASTED ON THE YOUNG (STORIES)

Rather than learn from their mistakes, though, soap execs compounded them in the mid-1990s. As the "youth demo" became more important to advertisers, young viewers dropped off. The 12-17 and 18-24 age groups were not being represented in soap viewers like they wanted. What the bosses should have done is beef up the stories of young moms and popular characters that current fans liked, adding a teen here and there to hook the kids of the moms who were watching.

Instead, they panicked and got rid of many of the veterans that had kept people watching all those years. In their place, soaps filled the screen with terrible newbie actors in stupid stories. Teens turned up on deserted islands, in mob stories, on the run, everywhere but with the adults they were related to that might have made fans care.

The worst slide occurred on "As The World Turns," after their famed head writer Doug Marland died suddenly in 1993. Marland had been the head writer of "General Hospital" during the heyday of Luke and Laura, head writer of "Guiding Light" during the stellar Nola Reardon/crazy Carrie Marler years, had created "Loving" with Agnes Nixon, and brought "As The World Turns" back to prominence after the firing of his former boss Irna Phillips. He refocused the Hughes family, created the Snyder family (which he based on his own) and scripted one of Daytime's most successful super couples in Lily and Holden, who went from two lovestruck teens in a barn to the caring parents of daytime's first gay core teen.

"He taught us all so much about soap opera," recalled Martha Byrne (Lily) to TV Guide's Michael Logan in a 2008 interview. "Doug would always say, 'You write a good story. You get good actors. That's all you need.' I remember when I joined the show [in 1985] the Oakdale police station was nothing more than a phone, a desk and a window. But you had Benjamin Hendrickson (Hal) and Hillary Bailey Smith (Margo, now 'One Life To Live's' Nora) and Scott Holmes (Tom) and Scotty Bryce (Craig). Man, were they good! And all anyone wanted to do was create great entertainment for the fans. Forget the fireworks and the tap dances. All we needed back then were good stories."

Unprepared to lose their prolific leader, "ATWT" went through a slew of writers and producers after Marland's death, each time decimating the cast and dismantling long-term story. Here's just one of the many inane stories told during this barely-watchable time: Teenaged Dani Andropoulos was sent to Oakdale by her mother Betsy to live with her great-grandmother, Ellen Stewart. (Betsy had been played by Meg Ryan in the 1980s. Shockingly, Ryan did not return to the show to deposit her daughter.) Dani made friends with fellow sudden teen Nikki, a child Hal Munson never knew he had. Dani and Nikki fought over two other high school strangers, Jeremy Wheeler and Ryder Hughes. Nikki made friends with a young WOAK intern named Terri and they started investigating another newcomer named David having set a fire in Chicago. Nikki found proof in David's Aunt Kathleen's house that David was adopted, she almost killed, got rescued by Hal, and was then grounded as punishment for her antics. Huh?

The absolute low point was when a character named Sarah Kasnoff decided to talk to her "inner child" in 1996 and the show did a split screen of this newbie actress talking to herself for an entire episode. I emailed *US Magazine's* Jennifer Lenhart, who was the "As The World Turns" editor at

Digest back in 1996, asking if she could remember any more details of that story.

She wrote back, "All I remember is you marching out of your office and handing me the labeled VHS tape so that I could pinpoint the exact beginning of the end of 'As The World Turns.'"It was all too stupid. "As The World Turns" forgot - or ignored - basic soap premises: 1) Not to make any sudden changes in a show that's been on the air for 40 years, and 2) The moms need to hook the daughters. But there was no need for the moms to watch their show after it was over-taken by a bunch of insipid soap teens walking around naval gazing, having unsafe sex, and chasing arsonists.

You can't really blame the revolving door of executive producers and head writers during these years for taking high paying jobs (over $1 million a year) in a field they knew noth-ing about, once they were offered. But where were the P&G execs being paid to oversee this show? How could they not step in?

Especially when Marland had left behind his own personal bible of what to do - and what not to do - when taking over a show. I know this because I conducted the last interview with Doug Marland before he died in 1993, and we got chatting about common mistakes soap writers make when they take over a show. Thank God the tape recorder was running.

We edited Doug's list after he died and published it posthumously in *Soap Opera Digest* as a guide from one of the true legends in the business. Here it is:

How Not To Wreck A Show

— By Douglas Marland

• *Watch the show*

• *Learn the history of the show. You would be surprised at the ideas that you can get from the backstory of your characters.*

• *Read the fan mail. The very characters that are not thrilling to you may be the audience's favorites.*

• *Be objective. When I came in to "ATWT," the first thing I said was, 'what is pleasing the audience?' You have to put your own personal likes and dislikes aside and develop the characters that the audience wants to see.*

• *Talk to everyone; writers and actors especially. There may be something in a character's history that will work beautifully for you, and who would know better than the actor who has been playing the role?*

• *Don't change a core character. You can certainly give them edges they didn't have before, or give them a logical reason to change their behavior. But when the audience says, "He would never do that," then you have failed .*

• *Build new characters slowly. Everyone knows that it takes six months to a year for an audience to care about a new character. Tie them in to existing characters. Don't shove them down the viewers' throats.*

• *If you feel staff changes are in order, look within the organization first. P&G does a lot of promoting from within. Almost all of our producers worked their way up from staff positions, and that means they know the show.*

• *Don't fire anyone for six months. I feel very deeply that you should look at the show's canvas before you do anything.*

• *Good soap opera is good storytelling. It's very simple.*

Marland's untimely death left a hole in the show that wasn't filled until Hogan Sheffer took over as head writer in 2000. Sheffer went on to win four Emmys, and "World Turns" enjoyed a brief renaissance. You could make the argument that those seven years of hack writers between Marland and Sheffer dealt a blow to "As The World Turns'" that they never recovered from. But in the end, it was Executive Producer Christopher Goutman and his protégé Ellen Wheeler that did in BOTH "As The World Turns" and "Guiding Light."

I got hooked watching with my mom, who got hooked watching with her mom. "ATWT" was my first love. Then the little girl across the street coerced me into coming over to her house to watch "All My Children." Well, in the beginning that might not have been the true reason I went to her house, but it became the reason I kept going back. Remember Jenny, Greg, Enid, Tad, Liza, Jesse, Angie, the false accusation of rape and New York? I sure do. It was hot, sweltering and summertime - and I didn't want to miss a beat.

Now, I watch Y&R. The genre of soaps has been very good to me. It bonded many generations of my family together. It taught me a lot about being neighborly and kind. It showed me it is okay to speak your mind as long as your heart is behind it.

And it reminded me that family is the most important thing out there.

- Mark Jenkins from Montgomery, Alabama

CHAPTER 12

Naming Names

The two oldest soaps "Guiding Light" and "As The World Turns" - both created by Irna Phillips - were canceled by CBS in recent years. What happened?

They were murdered.

First, let me say that I don't think the Executive Producers that brought them down, Ellen Wheeler and Chris Goutman are bad people; or that they purposely tanked Daytime's most revered soap operas. There were a series of dominoes that led to the downfall of both shows, including key people leaving, improper oversight from P&G which produced them, lack of promos and support from CBS, shoddy head writing, and a television marketplace that may simply have identified both shows too strongly as their "grandmother's soap." But having lived through their decline myself as an editor at two soap magazines, and interviewed pretty much every actor and behind the scenes person at both shows over the last two decades, I have to say that the colossal hubris and refusal to listen to ANYONE who contradicted them on the parts of both Goutman and Wheeler played a big part in the demise of both shows.

THE LIGHT DIMS

"Guiding Light's" downward slide began when Beverlee McKinsey abruptly quit the show in 1992. McKinsey joined "Guiding Light" as Alexandra Spaulding in 1984 after a wildly popular stint as Iris Carrington on sister show "Another World." She was long one of daytime's leading actresses, but did not suffer fools gladly. She let it be known after about eight years that she was unhappy with her story at "Guiding Light," when Alexandra was meddling in son Nick McHenry's romance with Mindy Lewis. But Executive Producer Jill Farren Phelps (now EP at "General Hospital") never thought McKinsey would walk.

"I had warned Jill that I was not happy with the storyline, although I don't think she paid attention to me," McKinsey told *Soap Opera Weekly's* Mark McGarry in 2000. (McKinsey died in 2008.) "I don't believe she'd read my contract; she was not aware that I could quit every six months. I said, 'I may just have to quit.' She said, 'You have a contract.' I said, 'You better read it.' I don't think she ever did. So she was really stunned when it happened."

McKinsey was required to give eight weeks' notice to get out of her contract. So, she scheduled her annual eight-week vacation, taped her last scenes, and then quit as she walked out the door.

"I didn't tell anybody in advance because I didn't want a big fuss made," downplayed McKinsey. "I didn't want a party. I just did my last scene and left. Plus, the last scenes were difficult scenes, and I wanted to be able to concentrate on that and not have to worry about anything else."

McKinsey confided her plans to her close friend David Loveless, who was "Guiding Light's" Costume Designer at the time, but swore him to secrecy.

"I told the head of wardrobe because he was already planning what he was going to buy for me for fall. One night at dinner I said, 'Don't buy anything, because this is what's happening.' Everybody was expecting me to leave that day. They just weren't expecting me to never come back."

The show recast with soap vet Marj Dusay the following year. She did yeoman work in the role, but it was never quite the same for fans. Yes, "GL" was at a creative high at the time - Harley/Mallet, Nick/Mindy, Ross/Blake (Sherry Stringfield), the Springfield Blackout, then Roger/Mindy - but there was a palpable hole where McKinsey had been.

Then came the next domino - killing longtime heroine Maureen Bauer in a car crash in 1993. Executive Producer Jill Farren Phelps has fallen on her sword and apologized for that decision many times, so we won't beat her up for it again here. She told me years ago that her mistake as a young EP was taking focus group information about leading "Guiding Light" characters and misreading the tepid response to

Maureen as viewers not caring about the character. It never occurred to the fans being polled that Maureen would ever go anywhere, so they focused their energy on villains like Alexandra Spaulding and Roger Thorpe.

Phelps mistakenly translated that as Maureen being expendable.

"Guiding Light" scripted a boffo exit for Maureen where she learned that her best friend, Lillian Raines, was having an affair with her husband, Ed Bauer. Maureen and Ed had a wrenching confrontation at the Bauer cabin after which Maureen stormed off. Her car skidded off the road and she was killed.

Maureen's portrayer, Ellen Parker, nailed every scene and won a Daytime Emmy for her work in 1993. What happened to daytime's oldest soap after that can best be described as death by a thousand cuts.

Respected veteran Paul Rauch ("Another World," "One Life to Live,""Santa Barbara") took over as EP of "Guiding Light" in 1996 and hired fellow vets Barbara Esensten and James Harmon Brown ("Dynasty," "The City") as head writers. In a bid to gain viewers, the new team tried to copy the outlandish stories that "Days of our Lives" was telling to

goose ratings (Marlena's possession, anyone?). They cloned

Reva Shayne in a ridiculous story involving Reva's frozen eggs

and the clone taking Reva captive. They also had Reva step

into a painting and travel through time.

"Days" fans were used to crazy tales, but "Guiding

Light" fans were not. Ratings fell further.

Note: One lovely thing Rauch did was bring former

"Search for Tomorrow" star Mary Stuart on to the show as Meta

Bauer. Meta had not been seen for two decades, but soon took on

a matriarchal role similar to the late Bert Bauer's. Stuart played

the role until her death in 2002.

Next, the show tried to copy "General Hospital," by

bringing the mob to town in the form of the Santos family,

and going to the fake island of San Cristobel, where Reva was

revealed to have been an amnesiac princess. She had given

birth to Prince Richard Winslow's son Jonathan, and forgot-

ten. Those attempts worked for a while because fans latched

on to couples like mobster Danny Santos and sweet Michelle

Bauer, and dashing Prince Richard and Reva's hardluck sister

Cassie. But ratings soon dipped again.

Enter John Conboy, who made his bones as Executive Producer of "Love Is A Many Splendored Thing," "The Young and the Restless," and "Capitol," and was known for his lush production values and great relationships with actors. Conboy cranked up super couple Gus and Harley, made the show edgier and amped up the look.

"Conboy had enthusiasm, and the audience was responding," says a long-time "Guiding Light" employee who asked not to be named since he still works in the industry. "But he was taking too much control of the show, so he rubbed Mickey the wrong way."

Mickey was Mary Alice Dwyer-Dobbin, a former ABC exec who fought the good fight most of her soap career, both at ABC and P&G. But she clashed with Conboy.

"Conboy spooked P&G because he started showing bare asses on the guys right after the whole Janet Jackson issue," continues the "Light" source, referring to Jackson's "wardrobe malfunction" at the January, 2004 Super Bowl where her breast was exposed.

"A week later we aired a scene with Shayne showing his ass and got in trouble with the FCC. John was too provocative, so he was out."

Unfortunately for "Guiding Light," Ellen Wheeler was waiting in the wings to take his job - and Dwyer-Dobbin was soon let go. Wheeler had been a successful actress in the 1980s on both "Another World" as Marley (where she was replaced by Anne Heche) and "All My Children" as the AIDS-stricken Cindy, winning Daytime Emmys for both roles. She had lived her own mini-soap opera by marrying her "Another World" co-star Tom Eplin (Jake) while they were working together, divorcing him, and then getting remarried to her second husband Shannon in a Mormon Church.

In the late 1990s, Wheeler parlayed her close friendship with former "All My Children" director Chris Goutman into a directing gig at "Another World," where he was Executive Producer. "Another World" was canceled in 1999. Goutman then took over as EP of "As The World Turns," hiring Wheeler there, too, as a director. With no one at the P&G soap wheel anymore, Goutman was able to convince P&G to hire Wheeler at sister show "Guiding Light" as an Associate Producer in 2002. Numerous sources told me she then spent the next two years undermining Conboy until

P&G ousted him in 2004 and she became Executive Producer.

"Ellen has been campaigning for his job the whole time, so she helped manufacture John's firing," affirms the source.

Faced with budget cuts, Wheeler hired a novice head writer named David Kreizman, cut back on the show's vets, and focused her energy on a young pair of first cousins - Reva's son Jonathan and Cassie's daughter Tammy - falling in love.

"Kreizman had a few good storylines in the beginning, but then no," says the source. "It wasn't all his fault. There was so much involvement, you couldn't get a good clean vision. Every story had to be approved by CBS and P&G and it became very watered down. It got to the point where any scene could be played by any character. There wasn't any personality to the stories anymore."

Indeed, the most interesting characters lost their individuality, and the popular actors started to leave.

"We turned a terrible corner when they broke up Reva and Josh and hooked him up with [her sister] Cassie," shudders the source. "Laura [Wright, Cassie] had found out about the storyline during her negotiations and said 'I don't want to play that.' Laura is a smart cookie. She knew the audience wouldn't buy it. So when "GH" came calling, she said, 'I'm outta here.' And we all said, 'This is going to kill the show.'"

Laura Wright joined "General Hospital" in 2005 as Sonny's volatile ex-wife Carly Corinthos, and things sunk further in Springfield.

"They started putting people together based on their contracts and what they were making," reveals the source. "So behind the scenes, you had P&G saying, 'You can only use Kim Zimmer [Reva] four times this month, because we don't want to go over her guarantee. And you can only use Justin Deas [Buzz] this much until his pay cycle comes up again.' They were crafting storylines around the way P&G said they could, based on the contracts and schedules of actors."

This meant that "Guiding Light's" popular veterans were rarely in scenes together, because it cost too much money. And yet, as every soap fan will tell you, those are the scenes people tune in for. Nobody cared when Josh was paired with a boring recast of Cassie, or when Harley (the popular Beth Ehlers) smooched a lame Australian named Cyrus Foley. Wheeler allowed beloved vets like Jerry ver Dorn (Ross) and Beth Ehlers (Harley) to slip away, and filled up the screen with recasts and sudden children of veteran characters, played by newbie actors who couldn't hold a candle to the originals. Do Daisy, Cyrus, Griggs, Rafe, Remy, Jeffrey, nuMallet, nuMarina ... ring a bell? I didn't think so.

That sound you hear is Irna Phillips rolling over in her grave.

"We constantly asked ourselves how Ellen kept her job, but I guess she kept the numbers in check," continues the source. "All P&G cared about was the bottom line. I think in a weird way Ellen *was* trying to nudge soaps forward and attract a younger audience. But she wouldn't listen to anyone, she was completely closed off to suggestions, and she couldn't admit it when she made a mistake - like those awful 'Wednesday Shows.'"

The "Wednesday Shows" were special episodes instituted by Wheeler that didn't have anything to do with the rest of the action on the show (um, hello, it's a *soap*). "Guiding Light" would spotlight one character each week, and then follow them through an entire episode. It was fine if it was Reva or Harley or Alan, or if something major happened on the episode (doctor visits were big), but unwatchable when it was some newcomer house hunting, or two snoozers leading up to their first kiss for an hour.

"Ellen and Dave thought they were great," marvels the source. "They kept doing them long after people said, 'Stop, they're not working.' One of the worst ones was that weird anniversary show for our 15,000th episode. They did this alternate reality where Reva bonked her head and all the characters were the opposite of what they were supposed to be. I mean, what was that?"

BYE BYE BAUERS

The final domino came in the form of a sleepy little New Jersey town called Peapack that knocked our beloved Springfield down for good. On February 29, 2008, Wheeler launched the new "production model" that was supposed to save "Guiding Light." Her plan was to use hand-held cameras, permanent sets, and location shooting to revitalize this 70 year-old jewel.

"We all knew about the house in Peapack way before they told us about it," says the source of the house in New Jersey that would soon be used for much of the show's action. "I remember a general meeting with everybody where Ellen allowed people to ask questions. Someone said, 'We're hearing rumors about a house the show has bought in New Jersey where we're all going to have to go work.' You could hear a pin drop. She said, 'No, that's not true at all.' Turned out we were just *leasing* the house."

For some reason, Wheeler shrouded her Peapack plans in secrecy, keeping them even from CBS.

"Everyone was going to [CBS Daytime Honcho] Barbara Bloom and begging her to do something, but she turned a blind eye. And Ellen flatly refused to release the scripts to anyone. Ricky Paull [Goldin, Gus] didn't want anything to do with Peapack, so he quit." (Goldin joined "All My Children" later that year as Tad's brother Jake Martin.)

Wheeler filmed the first "location" episode on the sly with only a handful of people. Numerous actors spoke off-the-record of the debacle that followed, but true to daytime's protective form did not want to be quoted - even though their show isn't even on anymore.

"I remember we had a special airing of the first episode in the studio," recalls an actor. "They called everybody in and brought in lunch. We all sat there and watched this horrible episode. There was no storyline, they just placed people in different sets, like Josh and Billy on a work site with Remy. Everyone politely clapped and then we all filed out going, 'Oh my God, what garbage.' Ellen was furious; it was like hell had frozen over. We found out later she wrote the episode herself."

Things went downhill from there, if you can imagine. Sources say CBS honchos finally got a look at what Wheeler was doing and did not like what they saw. The shaky cameras and rough production values were bad enough, but viewers often could not hear the dialogue.

"Our days were numbered after that," sighs the source. "But Ellen just stayed in her tunnel and plowed ahead. We turned real [executive] offices into nail salons and her office into a church sanctuary and shot everything with those awful hand held cameras. She loved all the technical stuff. She was more invested in that than the actual storyline and characters on the show, which of course was the problem. Her attitude was, 'How dare they not buy into my vision?'"

The cast had it the worst, changing their clothes on location shoots in cars and behind garages, and not getting proper hair, make-up or wardrobe. Contrary to what fans were seeing on air, it was still supposed to be a soap opera...

"I can't tell you how humiliating it was out there. I remember one chilly day we were shooting a scene of Dinah and Mallet playing golf. It was supposed to be May, so Gina [Tognoni, Dinah] wasn't wearing a coat. She was freezing and got cranky. Ellen took off her giant down coat with the big label on it and said, 'Just wear this, it's fine.' I thought the costume designer was going to die. She had no respect for her staff or the genre, and she disregarded the audience beyond belief. We'd all be out there and the director would ask a question and she'd say, 'Oh, the audience won't notice. They won't care.' Yes, they will. They're invested! They care!"

"Guiding Light" limped along for over a year with the new "production model" as the writing - and morale - deteriorated.

"Fans just want to see their favorite characters in a well-written storyline," laments the source, who has gone on to work on another show. "They don't care if they're sitting in a real diner. They just want to see what happens to them."

"Guiding Light" was canceled in March, 2009.

"No show in daytime or primetime, or anytime, has touched so many millions of viewers across so many years," said CBS daytime exec Barbara Bloom in a statement.

She was later ousted.

The last episode aired on September 18, 2009, a full 72 years after Irna Phillips dreamed up her enduring vision of a light in the window to guide Reverend Ruthledge's flock.

"I don't think P&G willingly got out of the soap biz," surmises the source. "The people in charge just didn't understand why people watch soaps, which kills me because that was their whole thing - marketing, and their connection to their buyers for 80 years. They lost contact with that."

AND THEN THE WORLD ENDED

Once "Guiding Light" went down, it was only a matter of time before P&G bailed on its last soap. As detailed earlier, "As the World Turns" was basically presumed dead for most of the 1990s. The show rebounded with the hiring of Head Writer Hogan Sheffer in 2000, who came on just after Christopher Goutman was hired as Executive Producer in 1999.

Goutman has long been known as one of the most talented directors in Daytime. He studied directing at Carnegie Mellon, moved to New York, and then ironically started getting hired as an actor. He played Marc D'Antoni on "Search for Tomorrow" in 1978-1979 (where he met his luminous wife Marcia McCabe, who played Sunny Adamson), Matt Sharkey on "The Edge of Night" from 1980-1981, and George St. John on the "Another World" spinoff "Texas" in 1982.

While acting on "The Edge of Night," Goutman informed Executive Producer Nick Nicholson that he had a degree in directing. Nicholson gave him a shot behind the camera, and Goutman never looked back. He spent the next 20 years directing almost all the New York-based shows: "All My Children," "As the World Turns," "Guiding Light," and "Another World."

Note: I went to Jamaica in 1996 with "All My Children" to cover the location shoot of Noah and Julia on the run after Noah was found guilty of murdering Julia's rapist, Louie. Chris Goutman was the director. He spent days waist-deep in water directing the fight scenes that lead to Taylor pushing Julia over the waterfall, and then tackled Hayley and Mateo's "From Here to Eternity" beach sex scenes. Some of the actors were not getting along at all, but you'd never know it from the amazing work Goutman put on the screen.

When "Another World" was on its last legs, Goutman was promoted from director to Executive Producer. "AW" went off the air in 1999. He then took over as EP of "As the World Turns," while also continuing to direct episodes. By most accounts, the early 2000s were a period of great creativity and rebirth at "World Turns." The show won four Daytime Emmys in five years for Outstanding Drama Series Writing Team (2001, 2002, 2004, and 2005), as well as taking the top prize for Outstanding Daytime Drama in both 2001 and 2003. Sheffer left in 2005. (He joined "Days of our Lives" in 2006 and now writes for "The Young and the Restless.")

But things started to turn at "World Turns" in the mid-2000's. With Dwyer-Dobbin out as the P&G exec overseeing the soaps, Goutman (along with his pal Ellen Wheeler at "Guiding Light") started taking more and more control - and becoming more removed.

"I really only saw 'Producer Goutman' a few times while I was at 'World Turns,'" recalls Hunt Block, who played Craig Montgomery from 2002 to 2005. "On days he was directing, sure. But otherwise, I think I was in his office maybe three times in five years. Once to get hired, once to get fired, and once for I don't know what."

Goutman started getting more involved in long-term story, and even casting. He replaced the popular Hunt Block with an old friend of his named Jeffrey Meek, who had the wrong look and energy for a sexy villain like Craig. Meek was soon let go. Craig was recast again with Scott Bryce, who had originated the role in the 80s, and then again with "General Hospital" star Jon Lindstrom. That was a lot of needless, unnecessary change for the show's most important bad guy.

Elsewhere, they created a web series called "InTurn" where "nine beautiful, ambitious young actors moved to NYC

to battle it out for a contract role on 'As the World Turns.'"
Much of the show's publicity efforts went into promoting this
web series full of nobodies. CBS VP of Daytime Programming Richard Mensing, who was the executive conduit to the
soaps, wrote a weekly blog about "InTurn" billed as "From
your guy on the InSide." Many thought Mensing should have
been focused more on what was still their bread and butter,
the P&G soaps - especially after Goutman hired failed "Guiding Light" head writer David Kreizman to come on board at
"World Turns."

And then came Martha.

Martha Byrne started playing the role of young heroine Lily Walsh in 1985 as a teenager. Her pairing with Jon
Hensley, who played brooding stable boy Holden Snyder, was
one of soap's most enduring match-ups. More importantly,
Byrne was an outspoken cheerleader for "World Turns," and
an unabashed fan of soap operas. Despite being the star of
the show, playing a dual role (Lily and Rose), winning two
Emmys, and having three kids, she was the go-to person for
charity events, fan luncheons, press interviews, you name it.

Note: I can't tell you how many times I was on deadline for my soap column in the New York Daily News and one of her co-stars hadn't called me. The publicist would say, "Let me try Martha..." and five minutes later the phone would ring. "What do you need?" she would say cheerfully.

So it was beyond shocking when the news came out in 2008 that Martha Byrne was leaving the show after 20 years. She took the high road, saying it was an amicable parting and she wished the show well.

But then Goutman issued a statement saying, "We made Martha an incredibly generous offer in hopes that she would remain a valuable member of the 'ATWT' cast. Unfortunately, Martha has decided to leave despite our best efforts to keep her."

That was his domino. Byrne then gave a few select interviews, including this scorcher to *TV Guide's* Michael Logan:

"This was the situation," she explained to Logan. "Last year, I was asked to take a tremendous pay cut, and I did so willingly because I love 'ATWT' and understood the financial situation the show was facing. I was willing to do anything to keep the show going, including giving up money, so we worked out a one-year contract. One year later, we go into this new contract negotiation. I had only one request and I wanted it on paper - that I would work the same amount of days this year that I did last year. I considered it a gesture of good faith on their part. I asked for nothing else."

Byrne was told they could not accommodate her request, which is a standard negotiating tactic while ironing out a new contract. But that same day, the show sent out what's called a "breakdown notice" inviting agents to submit actresses for a recast of Lily Snyder.

"That shouldn't happen in the middle of negotiations," Byrne told Logan. "After that, things went from bad to worse. I can't get into those details but it solidified my decision to leave the show. I never intended to speak about this, but I must after Chris put out that press release saying that they did everything they could to keep me. I do not feel that was the case - and I feel the fans deserve the truth."

No one at P&G or CBS stepped in to stop Goutman from ousting Byrne. Lily was recast with a perfectly fine actress named Noelle Beck who had played Trisha Alden years ago on "Loving," but she wasn't Lily.

I mean, it was like trying to recast Rachel on "Friends."

Fans were outraged and tuned out. Goutman adopted his pal Wheeler's attitude of head down, full steam ahead.

"You couldn't even mention Martha's name to him," says a former co-worker. "We would have these meetings about story ideas, location shoots, how to save the show, and all anybody wanted to say to him was, 'Bring Martha back!' But we couldn't."

Ratings sunk further. "As The World Turns" was canceled in December 2009, and aired its last episode on September 17, 2010.

"To Whom it May Concern," wrote one of the show's bereft actors on Facebook that day. *"Lack of fans or less cash to produce are not the reasons ATWT is over. (Did we REALLY need 3 seasons of InTurn?) Those of us who know the deal, cherish your love and support of the genre, and your contribution. You are ALL number one."*

AND THEN THERE WERE NONE

Neither Wheeler nor Goutman would speak of their show's demise to the soap press. However, Goutman did do an interview with a former writer for "As The World Turns" named Susan Dansby, who wrote a book called, *How Did You Get That Job?*

"Whatever I do in the future will be different," he said. "It will come nowhere near the sense of family, the sense of satisfaction, and the true pleasure of running a ship that has been for so many people a great source of comfort, entertainment, and part of their life. The pleasures have been indescribable, the satisfaction extraordinary. I will miss it."

When I went to Indiana University and pledged Kappa, I was thrilled to know that the other girls in the house loved the soaps. Every day, there was a huge group of girls sitting in the TV room watching ABC. Everyone loved to "hate" Erica Kane, and all her men were our heartthrobs.

The biggest adventure of all was Luke and Laura's wedding. It was standing room only in the sorority house. EVERYONE ditched classes. (I had friends who scheduled their entire semester's classes around "GH." Back then you didn't have VCR's and DVR's, so if you missed "GH," you had to rely on your best friend's description of what happened.)

The day Luke and Laura got married, every girl in the house was there. So was our housemom, the cooks and one of the waiters from the Optometry School. Everyone had Kleenex. A collective whoop went up when Luke kissed Laura. It was exhausting!

I have been hooked on the ABC shows ever since. When I go back to the Kappa house for reunions, memories of the soaps regularly come up. It was part of our "coming of age" - a way to break the stress of studying. We still talk about those characters as if they are part of our families.

I'm going to miss them desperately...

- **Sallie Jo Tardy Mitzell from Indianapolis, IN**

CHAPTER 13
The ABC's of Soaps: Kane was Able

ABC Daytime has had the strongest line-up in recent years for many reasons, but mainly because they have always owned their shows. That means they have never had to pay a licensing fee to a separate company for the privilege of airing them like CBS and NBC have to.

It also gave ABC more control over their shows, allowing them to do character crossovers between the soaps, and mass fan events like *ABC Super Soap Weekend* at Disney's Hollywood Studio in Orlando, FL. ABC also has had something no other network ever had: Susan Lucci.

She is, quite simply, the face of daytime.

Lucci joined "All My Children" as obstreperous teenage vixen Erica Kane when the show started in 1970 and has
represented everything fans love about soap operas ever since:
glamour, excitement, drama, and most importantly, continuity. Because Erica never left. She never backed down, never
gave in, never lost, even as she fought off rapists, romantic
rivals and bears. Sure, she had a series of severe romantic
disappointments, but she never stayed down for long. Erica
was the epitome of "I am woman, hear me roar," and millions
of viewers tuned in to watch her do just that, every day.

Lucci also believably shepherded Erica from teen to
ingenue to wife to mother to grandmother, allowing fans to
see the actress and character change and grow. The changes in
Erica reflected changes in the audience and in society, brought
to life every day by Lucci and the show's writers. In my opinion, the best thing to ever happen to Susan Lucci's career was
not winning that Emmy, because it made her relatable. Suddenly this gorgeous soap star with the strapping Austrian husband and two beautiful children was suffering a very public

disappointment year after year, with grace and dignity. The camera was square in her face as someone else's name was read 18 times, yet she smiled bravely, clutching husband Helmut Huber's hand every time.

I was at the Daytime Emmys in 1999 when Shemar Moore opened the Best Actress envelope and announced, "*The streak is over: Susan Lucci!*" The room went BERSERK. You could see Susan turning to Helmut and saying "Are you sure?" She could be forgiven for not quite believing the trophy was hers since someone else's name had been read every time before.

In addition to Lucci, the entire ABC lineup had the good fortune of its best, most popular actors not leaving over many decades. "All My Children's" Michael E. Knight (Tad), David Canary (Adam), Walt Willey (Jack); "One Life To Live's" Erika Slezak (Viki), Robin Strasser (Dorian), Robert S. Woods (Bo); "General Hospital's" Tony Geary (Luke), and until recently, the actors who played the Quartermaines were all in their jobs for 30-40 years.

That's iron-clad continuity, and the ABC shows wouldn't have been nearly as strong without it. Especially during the bad writing regimes, because these actors can make anything work.

They've had to.

WHEN IS AN ABORTION NOT AN ABORTION?

When some hack head writer at "All My Children" decided to rewrite one of the most groundbreaking events on Daytime and have Erica's 1973 abortion come to town as a grown man in 2005. Yes, soaps stretch credulity and yes, they take liberties with logic and truth, but that storyline was a violent slap in the face to every long-term fan, as well as to all the viewers who were proud that Agnes Nixon had taken such a bold stand for women's rights.

In the ill-advised rewritten story, a doctor named Greg Madden came to town, who Erica somehow figured out had performed her long-ago abortion during her marriage to Jeff Martin. She soon learned that Greg's son, Josh, was actually her own aborted fetus, which the mad doctor had re-implanted into his own wife. Yeah, *okay.*

Fans despised the story. It didn't help that Erica's 32-year-old abortion was somehow now only 24 years old; or that every time he turned around he had a new profession. He's a doctor! He's a pilot! No, he's a terminated pregnancy from the 70s.

"All My Children" made a lot of mistakes like that in the 2000s, underestimating their audience and abusing their loyalty. Fan erosion naturally occurred, leading to the show's cancelation in April, 2011. That sound you hear is the collective uproar of "AMC's" 2.5 million fans shouting "No!"

Behind the scenes, "AMC" had a perfectly nice executive producer named Julie Carruthers from 2003-2011, but she unfortunately had trouble staying within budget, and for some reason let every head writer walk all over her. Megan McTavish and Chuck Pratt were the two worst offending head writers, churning up so much ridiculous and disturbing plot for Pine Valley that there was no time for any emotional fallout from the big "events." There was a fire or earthquake every few months, but characters just dusted themselves off and went right back to their lives.

"Viewers don't care about the explosion," asserts longtime "AMC" star Thorsten Kaye (Zach). "They care about what happens after the explosion. How did it affect the characters they love? Who was changed by it?"

DEATH BY PANCAKE

The worst was Dixie's senseless, syrupy demise.

In 2008, actress Cady McClain (Dixie) went to "AMC" head writer Megan McTavish with some very real concerns about her character and storyline. Next thing you knew, Dixie was eating her "favorite" peanut butter pancakes (which she had never eaten before) in the Chandler living room, and the peanut butter had been poisoned in an attempt to kill JR's wife, Babe. Dixie clutched her throat and fell to the ground.

Stories like that that are what slowly eroded "AMC." It made no sense that ABC honcho Brian Frons would give head writers like McTavish and Pratt carte blanche to slowly dismantle the show.

Let's say they made an executive decision to kill 20-year heroine Dixie Martin. Maybe McClain made too much money, or "AMC" wanted the dramatic impact from her death. Fair enough.

What you DON'T do is throw Dixie's death away on two scenes of Dixie eating poison pancakes that the "Satin Slayer" meant for Babe, and then demean her by making her *share a funeral.* That was a gigantic slap in the face that said to every "AMC" fan:

"We don't care that you invested 20 years in this character. She's out."

We all know that Dixie's death came about because McClain complained about her character to McTavish, and McTavish retaliated by killing Dixie in the most insulting way she could conjure. That's where Brian Frons should have stepped in and said, "If you are determined to kill a legacy character, convince me why. And then make it *count* if you do. What are Adam, Tad, and JR's stories out of this? What do fans get from it? Where's the payoff?"

I mean, a payoff besides McTavish getting the momentary pleasure of punishing an actress for speaking her mind... before McTavish was fired herself.

LIZA WITH A HUH?

Here's how you can tell when an exec doesn't get

it: When "AMC" recast Liza, formerly played by clean cut blonde Marcy Walker, with sultry redhead Jamie Luner. Disparate looks aside, Luner is 15 years younger than the actors who play Tad, Jesse and Angie; Liza's high school classmates. There goes any hope of believably reminiscing about high school or playing any of Liza's backstory, which is the essence of all good soap tales.

There are so many other roles Luner could have played (Brooke's daughter Laura, Dixie's sister Melanie, Tad's ex Hillary, a new character) that weren't indelibly marked on the show like Liza was. Every time someone calls this 35-year-old redhead "Liza" or refers to her past with Tad, it's like being hit on the head with the recast mallet all over again. I prefer to think that the mistake reflects the fact that some new boss just didn't understand Liza's popularity, rather than any purposeful destruction, but it's so jarring you have to wonder.

Like Zarf. Remember him/her? The transgendered rock star who joined the show in 2006? His first scenes were sitting naked on the floor of Fusion's professional offices, where Erica, Bianca, Kendall and Greenlee worked.

Let's say you want to take fans on the journey of a man transitioning to become a woman, which an Agnes Nixon soap was perfectly positioned to do. Once you make that person so disrespectful as to introduce themselves to a room full of strangers naked in their work place, the preposterousness takes over and you lose what could have been meaningful rooting value.

The show also became all about hiring models as actors, recasting veterans with better looking people, and insulting actors when their contracts were up with lowball offers that made them quit.

"It isn't about the money, it's about being fair," said one big-named actor who left the show in 2010. "They're cutting benefits for camera people, slashing salaries, and then paying one or two ass-kissing stars top dollar." *Note: This person is not referring to Lucci, who took a pay cut.*

Or Thorsten Kaye, whose popular Zach was written off in 2010. Previously, no one has ever told the real story of what happened there, so here goes: When the show moved to California in 2009, Kaye said he was willing to commute. But Alicia Minshew, who plays Zach's wife Kendall was on a nine-month maternity leave, and "AMC" told Kaye they could not come up with a story for Zach without Kendall, so he couldn't work either. (I know, *what*?!)

So Kaye bided his time. Then, "AMC" said he had to commit to moving to California and sign a two-year deal. Kaye, whose partner Susan Haskell was playing "One Life To Live's" Marty in New York at the time, said he couldn't commit to five days a week for two years with his family (including two young daughters) living on the east coast, but would commute and find a way to make it work. Despite the fact that Susan Lucci was commuting, "AMC" said no to Thorsten Kaye and ousted him before his current contract was even up, claiming to the fans that it was "his choice."

"I was surprised they let me go six months early, because I felt like I could have helped them," acknowledges Kaye.

Zach perished in a plane crash in November 2010 (yes, in true soap fashion, his luggage eventually washed up on shore). Once again, fans were outraged at the senseless exit of another popular veteran. Ratings fell 36% year over year.

ALL MY PROBLEMS

And then "All My Children" was canceled. I asked a behind-the-scenes person at "AMC" to help explain the downward spiral.

"Julie Carruthers might be a lovely person but she is NO EP," he responded. "The hack writers did so much damage. Killing Dixie because the actress blasted the head writer in private to her face, stupid plotlines that didn't work getting trotted out again and again, and don't forget the 'un-abortion.' The costly relocation to the studio in LA situated near the headquarters of the Bloods and the Crips and conveniently close to at least three porn studios didn't save the show any money. The actors on the show and the fans of the show deserved better than the terrible writers and the last Executive Producer of 'AMC.' It was pathetic to see what the crown jewel in Daytime was reduced to. Everyone was either cast aside or told they're replaceable. This never would have happened under [former honchos] Angela Shapiro or Mickey Dwyer-Dobbin."

Insiders were not surprised when "AMC" got canceled - they had been watching the show disintegrate for years.

What shocked everyone was that the higher-rated, lower-cost, creatively top-shelf "One Life To Live" was canceled along with it.

ONE SHOW TO LOSE

How is it possible that "OLTL" got canceled, when it was the ONLY soap that gained viewers year over year? And it beat "GH" and "DAYS" in the ratings the week of April 4-8, 2011 when the decision was being made?

Total Viewers (+/- last week/last year)

1. *Y&R* 4,563,000 (-179,000/-770,000)

2. *B&B* 2,827,000 (-82,000/-426,000)

3. *OLTL* 2,630,000 (+56,000/+150,000)

4. *GH* 2,605,000 (-115,000/-163,000)

5. *DAYS* 2,363,000 (+135,000/-354,000)

6. *AMC* 2,303,000 (-80,000/-123,000)

If the point of the soap replacement shows is to "provide enormous opportunity for the creation of ancillary businesses and growth," as Brian Frons stated in his press release, isn't that exactly what "OLTL" did? Its lead-in, "AMC," was down 123,000 viewers, and yet, "OLTL" was up 150,000 viewers year to year. It was the ONLY soap opera showing growth. Not only do I not understand this decision from a fan or ABC brand loyalty point of view, I don't get it from a business standpoint either – not ABC's or other cable stations.

According to a March 2011 article in *The Week*, the ratings for Oprah Winfrey's new network OWN are about 10 percent lower than they were for Discovery Health, the channel OWN replaced. *The Week* estimated that OWN averages 135,000 viewers, and only 45,000 of them are in the target demo of women ages 25 to 54. Naturally, viewers bombarded fellow soap fan Oprah with their pleas for her to take the ABC soaps, which would have been win/win for the soaps *and* her struggling network.

Look, I love Oprah and I watch OWN. The "Oprah: Behind the Scenes" are fantastic, but the other content on OWN consists of 1) Talk shows starring Oprah's friends, 2) Old movies starring Oprah's friends, and 3) Reality shows starring Oprah's friends. Oprah could use a little scripted original content, never mind 20 times more people watching her network.

DOPE AND CHANGE

"*I'm pissed off,*" wrote former "OLTL" star Catherine
Hickland on her blog a few days after "One Life To Live"
was canceled. "*Do I think this know-nothing [ABC exec] owes
anyone a job? No I do not. Do I think the man owed people
who gave ALL for all of those years a little respect? YES. "The
ratings kept declining" he will spin. That was the plan, wasn't
it? Isn't that what you have been doing with all of your character
assassinating and lame story telling? Isn't that what you've been
doing micromanaging your producers, writers, and staff to insan-
ity? Business 101 teaches you to hire super competent people and
let them do their job. Control freaks find this nearly impossible,
which is why they ultimately fail. It's pure arrogance to think
that you know what the audience will accept on shows that they
know far better than you do. They didn't accept mediocrity, and
for that the viewers were punished.*"

"AMC's" stories have indeed been mediocre, but
"OLTL's" have not, so it's especially hard to fathom why ABC
would throw that high-quality soap baby out with the Pine

Valley bath water. If it was a question of money, they could have easily lowered the budget in ways that would not have impacted the air shows and jarred viewers.

"I understand that they have to cut costs and change the show, that's fine," offers Kaye. "But give the audience some continuity, something to root for. People want hope, fantasy, escape; not hospitals and dead babies. If you don't give them what they want, then you can't be upset that they are leaving."

ABC was in the best position to give fans what they want, because they own their shows and could turn on a dime. Where they went wrong was in hiring network execs who didn't understand why people watch soaps in the first place. It's not about numbers and demos, it's about love and passion. Viewers have a connection to their soaps that they will *never* have to talk shows, game shows, judge shows, or mark my words, the cooking show and weight-loss show slated to replace "AMC" and "OLTL." Soaps are in living rooms across America every single day, watched devotedly either in real time on the networks, on DVR or at night on SOAPnet. They are a *destination*.

Execs that don't understand that - or even get why people watch soaps - need to find another line of work. But soaps are also a business, and they have to make money. So let's take a look at all the ways they could be doing that today.

As Kelly Ripa likes to say, "You're welcome, America."

CHAPTER 14

How to Save Soaps: Go Back to Basics

Everything we need to know about how to run a successful daytime drama TODAY, we learned from Irna Phillips and her protégés Agnes Nixon, Bill Bell, and Doug Marland. Let us count the ways…and show the way to get back on track.

PRODUCT PLACEMENT

Irna created the soap opera in 1930 specifically for product tie-ins, so where are they?

At a time when Sherri Shepherd is singing songs about Charmin while lying on top of a piano on "The View," and Tina Fey is cracking wise about Slankets and Snapple while getting money for product placement on "30 Rock," how is it possible that the soaps, who invented that, aren't doing it?

Picture a scene at the local groovy bar on every soap.

Victor Newman storms into Glow Worm on "The Young and the Restless," and orders "Stoli, neat. And don't mess it up with any fruit." Soaps' most fashionable characters are recovering alcoholics. How is San Pellegrino or Diet Coke not a regular staple at all the clubs? Erica Kane, Nikki Newman and Katherine Chancellor could keep Perrier in business all by themselves.

What happens when "The Young and the Restless" housekeeper Esther is unable to get the stains out of Murphy's clothes after he goes fishing? What kind of mascara does "Days of our Lives'" crybaby Chloe use that never seems to run? How is it possible that there isn't a signature drink all the time at "All My Children's" Confusion bar made with V8 V-Fusion? They tried a V8 tie-in a few years ago as part of the "Go Red for Women" campaign, but the writers didn't even try to tie V-Fusion to the bar, and the writing was so forced, it was laughable.

"Remember that?" laughs Thorsten Kaye (Zach). "'Did you drink your juice?' 'Yes, did you?' 'Yes. It sure was delicious!' Product placement is, 'Hey, you look good in Armani.' 'Thank you.' Or, 'What are you eating?' 'Campbell's Soup. It's pretty good.' 'Huh, Sonny's eating the soup. Maybe I'll try it.' Just make it seamless, part of the story. In James Bond movies, great cars get wrecked. You're not going to not buy an Aston Martin because it got wrecked, it's a great looking car. You don't have to hit people over the head. They get it."

Hitting people over the head has been soaps' biggest problem with product placement in recent years. When "Guiding Light" was on its last legs, Procter & Gamble ordered them to start placing P&G products in scenes, but wouldn't provide the products to the show.

"The prop shopper had to actually go out and buy cans of Pringles to accommodate the request," marvels a former staffer. "We all shook our heads and said, 'Why are you out buying Pringles?' 'Because we have to use them and no one is giving them to us.' I remember one scene in a van where someone whipped out a can of Pringles and passed it around. There's nothing wrong with that. We just rolled our eyes, because we couldn't believe we had to go out and buy them."

The way for product placement to work is to integrate it into the action the same way Irna Phillips did 80 years ago. Recent attempts haven't worked, because it was obvious the writers were not on board with the effort and therefore the scenes were clumsily written. Here's the bottom line: that is how soaps started and that is a big way that they can be saved. But the writing must be clever, and the shows must embrace it. It's not a "come down" to throw Tropicana into a scene if it saves 300 jobs and keeps your show on the air.

Get over it.

CUT THE CAST

"I think soaps have to cut the number of actors on contract," offers Hunt Block, who was on contract on five different soaps including "As The World Turns" and "Knots Landing." "Have 10-15 contract and make the rest recurring. Have 'special guest stars' rotate in and out with your regulars."

That would save money and keep storylines from being based on questions like, "Who's under their guarantee?" Because as we learned from "Guiding Light's" demise, you need to play your vets if you want people to tune in.

Take "General Hospital." Your contract roles could be Sonny, Carly, Jason, Sam, Alexis, Robin, Patrick, Lucky, Liz, Michael, Lulu and Dante. Luke rotates in and out now, so that's the model. When there's a big mob hit, you crank up Sonny's henchmen along with Mac and the police force. When there's a bus crash, up comes the hospital staff: Steve Jr., Monica, Bobbie, Epiphany. When Sonny has a big trial, here comes Diane, Max and Milo to help Alexis clear him.

The basic number of contract players could fluctuate, but you get the idea. This guarantees a smaller nut of actor-related expenses, and could offer a wider array of players in the end.

FIX THE RATINGS SYSTEM

Currently, the soap cable channel SOAPnet airs five of the six soap operas three times overnight and during a marathon over the weekend. Yet, Nielsen doesn't count those eyeballs towards the ratings of the shows! They only count the actual live network viewing and same-day watching of the soaps. That's millions of people watching soaps and not being counted.

You'd think the networks would fight harder to keep track of whose watching their shows. Four and a half million people watched "The Young and the Restless" every weekday in April, 2011, and that doesn't even count those who recorded and watched it over 24 hours later - or the *millions more* who watched it on SOAPnet. Meanwhile, the fantastic 1960s-era nighttime soap "Mad Men" is lucky to crack 3 million viewers total, and it's a critical darling. Jimmy Kimmel logs 700,000 viewers at night on ABC and is considered a hit, while "All My Children" has more than three times that number during the day and isn't.

HUH?!

Why don't the networks value those viewers? I don't get it.

And don't get me started on the 18-49 demos being the most valuable. Most 18-year-olds I know don't have any money. And the people I know in their 50s spend tons of money, not just on trying every new toothpaste whitener on the market, but big-ticket items like cars and renovated kitchens and vacations. NBC recently did a study of people 55 to 64 showing they spend more than the average consumer on home improvement, large appliances, casual dining, cosmetics, electronics and digital devices like iPods and iPads.

There's gold in them thar (over the) hills!

When SOAPnet goes away in 2012, everyone will have to watch and/or record their shows live on the networks when they air. That will count towards daytime ratings. I predict a big bump, actually. That will prove that the business model for how the networks measure daytime ratings needs a complete overhaul.

AY, DIOS MIO

How is it possible that Spanish soap operas are thriving, yet American soap operas are not? Oh yeah, they focus on love and romance, not mobsters and dead babies. Let's learn a lesson from Spanish soaps like "La Reina del Sur" on Telemundo and go back to a little Love in the Afternoon. While we're at it, let's hire a Spanish soap opera star to draw some of the 45 million Hispanics currently living in the U.S. to the American soaps. If you get even 10% of them, you'll be the number one show.

GO BACK TO RADIO

Why aren't soaps simulcast on Sirius Radio? Soaps needs to be made more accessible to busy people leading busy lives. Podcasts, soaps on tape, maybe even reruns on an eager cable station. They could package classic episodes of "Guiding Light," hosted by real-life firecrackers Kim Zimmer and Michael O'Leary (Reva and Rick), who could introduce the action and then give funny comments. Ditto for "As The World Turns," with Martha Byrne (Lily) and Michael Park (Jack). The shows could be sponsored by a P&G product (hey, better late than never) and air in the middle of the night. Fans could DVR and watch later, the sponsor gets love from fans thrilled to revisit their show, and a little piece of Oakdale, Springfield and Bay City lives on.

SOCIAL MEDIA

I had drinks with an exec at ABC Daytime about 2-3 years ago and gave him a whole bunch of ideas about how to use social media to plug his soap lineup. I suggested creating a Facebook page for all the major soap characters and then doing status updates based on that day's action. How cool would it have been if "GH's" Sonny Corinthos had a Facebook page with posts like, "Jax had better watch out today," or "Carly sure is looking good on the back seat of that limo…"

I also recommended Twitter accounts for the ABC soap characters, where they could do the same thing – plug the upcoming on-screen action.

The exec responded that ABC would need to pay each show's writers if they were going to do that, and it wouldn't be worth it.

Fast forward to today, where fans have created fake Facebook pages for pretty much every soap character, and write the most outrageous things on these pages. ABC has no control over what is said, and none of it plugs their shows. They lost control of their brand across all forms of social media because they didn't want to try something new. How much money has been spent on ABC's daily promos over the last few years? This idea would have cost nothing.

LET THERE BE (ONE) LIGHT!

Use one vision for the shows. Hire a good, non-recycled head writer who loves the genre and let THEM tell the stories

"I heard a story about Irna Phillips once, when she was dictating 'Guiding Light' scripts out of the Drake Hotel [in Chicago]," recalls Shawn Dudley. "She made the decision to have Meta Bauer shot as she was pacing in her hotel suite. It just spilled out of her - she even shocked her own assistant! She loved it so much, she made it compelling. So when you're listing your dominos, or whatever the tipping point was, I would say when execs took control of the stories away from the head writers. That certainly took hold in the last few years of 'Guiding Light.'"

Bill Bell, one of the most successful head writers in daytime history, would most definitely agree. He revealed to the Museum of Broadcasting how meetings with Irna and P&G execs used to go in that Drake hotel suite.

"Irna and I would present our story thrusts for the months ahead," described Bell. "There would be comments, suggestions, discussions about new characters and old. In short, very stimulating meetings." The P&G execs "never once mandated that writers develop stories that didn't excite them or ones that in any way they had misgivings about. They realized what so many producers and network executives don't: that a head writer worthy of the name knows his characters and story better than anyone."

Those were the days.

CHAPTER 15

Where the Art is Today

S oap operas are in a precarious situation with the networks, which is maddening, absurd and unnecessary.   Millions of Americans with disposable incomes tune in every day to see what their favorite soap characters are up to.   They invite these people into their living rooms like old friends, hang on their every word, and discuss the goings-on with friends on Facebook and in chat rooms all over the Net.

This is not the case with any other form of programming. And yet shows like "Jimmy Kimmel Live," "Mad
Men," "The Daily Show," etc., which have lower ratings than
most soaps, are considered hits. Stephen Colbert would *kill*
for "All My Children's" ratings, so how is it possible that ABC
would even consider canceling the show?

I don't get it, and I am a trained professional. So, I
wrote to Anne Sweeney, the President of the Disney/ABC
Television Group, before the cancellations. I encouraged all
of the 5+ million fans of "All My Children" and "One Life To
Live" to do the same. Here's my letter, as posted on the *Soap
Opera Digest* website in April, 2011:

AN OPEN LETTER TO ANNE SWEENEY

*There are a lot of rumors flying around about
ALL MY CHILDREN and ONE LIFE TO LIVE,
which has millions of ABC soap fans very uneasy. It's
inconceivable to us that those shows might actually get
canceled, but just in case that idea is under consider-
ation, please allow me to argue in favor of two of the
most valued jewels in the entire Disney crown.*

You cannot underestimate the passion that ABC fans have for your entire soap lineup. Anyone who ever watched Erica Kane fend off a bear, Viki and Dorian compete for Mayor, or Luke pull off another jewel heist has a warm place in their hearts for all your soaps. Talk shows, game shows, judge shows and reality shows will never inspire the kind of loyalty that you currently enjoy today with your long-running soap operas. They are a DESTINATION for us. Yesterday's action informs today, which informs tomorrow - hopefully for a long time to come.

As a result, we tune in early to our local noon news shows, and stick around for Oprah and the 5:00 news. The ABC affiliates reap the benefit of our loyalty to your soaps every day. Oprah and Regis leaving your lineup will bring a lot of unwelcome change for viewers in 2011. The ABC soaps will be the only constant that ABC fans - and your affiliates - can count on.

And have you ever noticed how many promos ABC airs for its prime time lineup during the day? DANCING WITH THE STARS, THE BACHELOR,

*DESPERATE HOUSEWIVES, new series like BODY
OF PROOF starring former soap star Dana Delany
(LOVE OF LIFE, AS THE WORLD TURNS) - who do
you think is watching these shows? Soap fans, of course.
You hook us with the promos and make us tune in at
night to see what happens.*

*Speaking of tuning in at night, I am also a
big Jimmy Kimmel fan but I don't understand why his
700,000 viewers would be more valuable to you than
over twice that number watching each one of your three
soap operas.*

*Women are the decision makers in the household.
We buy everything from the toothpaste to the clothing
to the furniture, and usually the beer, too. We also have
a say in the cars and vacations. Why aren't our dollars
being targeted? We are a valuable group with money to
spend, and strong opinions on how to do that.*

*I also don't think our numbers are properly
represented in your ratings. If I watch ONE LIFE TO
LIVE every night on SOAPnet, I am not counted in any
list of people 1) enjoying your show or 2) watching your*

ads. If you are seriously considering getting rid of a soap,

at least wait till February 2012 when SOAPnet goes off

the air, and all your viewers will be watching or DVRing

their soaps on ABC Daytime where their numbers will

be counted. Better yet, test my theory and pull the soaps

off SOAPnet's same day viewing for a week. I think the

increased ratings will happily surprise you.

Finally, please don't underestimate brand loyalty.

ABC soap fans take our kids to the latest Disney movie

and watch Hannah Montana and paid $125 a ticket

to see "The Lion King" on Broadway and go on Disney

Cruises and have been to both Disneyland and Disney

World. It's all part of the same warm, fuzzy package to

us, one line from Simba to Susan Lucci.

ONE LIFE TO LIVE is currently the best soap

on the air. Watch it for a week and you'll be entertained,

inspired and moved. ALL MY CHILDREN needs

work, but new head writer Lorraine Broderick is the per-

fect person to whip it back into dramatic shape. A few

creative tweaks, and AMC will bounce back better than

Erica Kane after a short marriage.

Regardless, we will hang in, day after day, year

after year - because we are faithful soap fans inspired by

the heroines that your talented writers and execs put on

TV every day.

Living in hope that tomorrow will be a better

day.

Thank you for your time,

Carolyn Hinsey

Soap Opera Digest

That summed up how I felt then, and feel now, as I

know it does millions of other fans, including "AMC" loyalist

Oprah Winfrey, who just did a whole hour on the importance

of soap operas during her precious last 25th season. If you

don't believe me and Oprah, here is an email I received from

one of my "Opinionators" named Jackie. She sent it to my

Facebook soap page (CarolynOpinionHinsey). Jackie was a

fan of "Guiding Light" and did not take her show's cancella-

tion lightly.

"CBS is off my programming since they took GL off the air," she wrote. "No Sweet 16 [college basketball]. I accidentally taped the Neil Diamond concert last year and watched it before I realized it was on CBS. I am using up the last of my Crest toothpaste. I am also doing that to Tide. I watch my local weather on CBS cuz I worked with the weather man in college. That is 20 minutes of CBS a day. Seriously, that is all. And no P&G products newly purchased either. What little Y&R I watch, I catch on SOAPnet. ABC would be really hard for me to not watch… DWTS, OLTL, GH, CASTLE… but I'll do it if I have to."

Do you know how much energy it takes to look up all of P&G's products and then make a concerted effort to not buy them?

These people aren't kidding.

REALITY SHMEALITY

Networks are sadly mistaken if they think reality TV will ever replace soap operas.

The difference between soaps and reality shows like "Jersey Shore" and "The Real Housewives Of Anywhere" is that people may watch them for a limited time, but it's mostly to laugh at the antics of drunk overtanned people whose lives are train wrecks for hire. Soaps have heroes and heroines, good guys win, evil is not rewarded in the end, and what goes around comes around 100% of the time. Reality shows never go anywhere, except in circles. You can always tell when some producer told someone to pick a fight. It's orchestrated.

So let's take the temperature of the six remaining shows as of Summer 2011, assuming that smart execs + millions of fans = keeping them on the air for a long time.

GENERAL HOSPITAL

Pros: Very strong main cast and supporting players. Eg: Alexis, Diane, Spinelli, Max and Milo work for Sonny but could carry an entire episode on their own. Cast and show has won many Emmy awards in recent years. Tony Geary's flawed, self-loathing Luke remains the center of the show 32 years after he raped Laura on the dance floor. Couples like Sonny/Carly, Jason/Sam, Lucky/Liz and Patrick/Robin are still doing a strong, ongoing dance.

Cons: Nicknamed "Mob Central" because there is too much focus at times on Sonny, Jason, and the violent underworld. Gutting the beloved Quartermaine family was a mistake. So was turning whole shows into "The Brenda Hour," but with Vanessa Marcil leaving, that pendulum should swing back to the love story of Sonny and Jason where it belongs...

Prognosis: Excellent. "GH" is the jewel in the entire ABC Daytime crown.

Suggested Improvements: Maurice Benard (Sonny), Laura Wright (Carly) and Steve Burton (Jason) are among "GH's" many terrific actors who can carry anything - give them more comedy! Since the mob rules the town, bring back Anna and Robert Scorpio to run the police station. Resurrect Stuart Damon as Alan Quartermaine and crank up his war-of-the-roses marriage with Leslie Charleson's Monica. I don't care that Alan is dead, make it happen.

DAYS OF OUR LIVES

Pros: Bo and Hope are eternally ageless and still in trouble.
Enduring villain Stefano DiMera is still the strangely-accented
straw that stirs the Salem drink. "Days" boasts the cutest,
ahem, mature couple on all of daytime in Maggie Horton and
Victor Kiriakis, still played after all these years by Suzanne
Rogers and John Aniston (yes, Jennifer's father). Missy Reeves
is back as Jennifer Horton in a promising romance with
Shawn Christian's dreamy Daniel. There is a gay story said to
be coming down the pike that should draw buzz and interest.

Cons: Stories are taking a dumb turn with Stefano brain-
washing Rafe and putting a doppelganger in his place, and
Dr. Carly Manning shooting herself up with drugs in the
hospital, to name just two. There are too many young characters and few of them can act, including Rafe's boring and
unnecessary family.

Prognosis: Good. Anything is better than reruns of "The
Real Housewives of Whatever County" which NBC currently
airs in place of our beloved (sniff!) "Another World."

Suggested Improvements: Boot the no-talent kids. And I get that Deirdre Hall and Drake Hogestyn (Marlena and John) are huge stars and maybe "Days" can't afford them anymore. But there's a huge hole in the show where John and Marlena used to be, and they have kids all over the place. How are they not at weddings, christenings, murder trials? Strike a deal with the actors to be "special guest stars" from time to time and keep Salem feeling like *Salem*. It worked for Rosemary Prinz when Agnes Nixon brought the former "As The World Turns" star over to "All My Children" for the show's first six months, so why not?

ONE LIFE TO LIVE

Pros: Viki's DID, her daughter Jessica's DID (oops), Dorian's marriage to the younger David, Clint's flaws as a man, Bo's flaws as police commissioner, Nora's flaws as his wife, Blair's flaws with everything, John McBain's pain (this means you, Natalie), Todd, nuTodd, Rex, Gigi, Starr... you name it and "OLTL" has showcased it or shined a light on it. The humor on this show is outstanding – you could chop whole scenes out of it and think you were watching a sitcom. I could never do justice to David's ad campaign for a hemorrhoid remedy called "Have A Seat," but suffice it to say it *inflamed* everyone in Llanview.

Cons: Sorry, the Ford brothers are just the torsos that ate Llanview. Hot and sexy is one thing. Waxed and completely untrained is another. All the other actors chew these poor boys up in scenes, and their silly stories are simply not worth the carnage. Focus on your strengths, which is the entire rest of the show.

Prognosis: Should be excellent, but "OLTL" is slated to go off the air in January, 2012. If it does, that will only mean that ABC refused to admit that it made a mistake in moving "AMC" to LA and needed to cancel both shows to save face. That would be a needless, cowardly error.

Suggested Improvements: Recasting Cole and keeping his parents Patrick and Marty around would be an excellent start. I know it's selfish to want Tuc Watkins (David) to work less on "Desperate Housewives" and more on "OLTL," but there

- I said it.

ALL MY CHILDREN

Pros: Former head writer Lorraine Broderick was brought back in April 2011 to take the show off the air in September, 2011. One thing show killer David Kreizman (he took "GL" and "ATWT" off the air, and was let go from "AMC") did right was the Angie/Jesse baby swap story. I don't hate Tad's green card marriage to newbie Cara, either, because it cranks up Tad, Jake and Amanda. *Always tell stories with people fans care about. It's Soaps 101...* oh, never mind.

Cons: Enough with the marriages! Erica is best when she's feisty and strong, so put her front and center and let the men fight over *her*. Too many new people are eating screen time. No one cares about Griffin and his lame Robin Hood attempts to steal drugs from the rich and give them to the poor, or his smoldering passion for the Widow Slater who lost her husband Zach last Tuesday. Zach's murder mystery, complete with cartoon villains and terrible acting, turned out to be dumber than Dixie's death by pancake, and that's saying something.

Prognosis: Very grave.

Suggested Improvements: "AMC" is bringing back Cady McClain as Dixie and Thorsten Kaye as Zach just in time to end the show. If they had done that earlier, of course, they might not have gotten canceled. I also wouldn't mind Marj Dusay back as David's mother Vanessa so Erica would have someone to tangle with. Vanessa's other son Leo was played by the nicest guy you'd ever want to meet, Josh Duhamel, who is also on his way back for what we all hope is a big story.

THE YOUNG AND THE RESTLESS

Pros: Maria Arena Bell, protégé and daughter-in-law of legendary creator William J. Bell, is head writer and executive producer of this show, which has been #1 for 22 years in a row. Her family (Hi, the Bells) still owns a big piece of it; her husband, William J. Bell, Jr. oversees the show. Hopefully, no one is messing with Maria's stories or vision, which was her late father- in-law's cardinal rule. Victor, Nikki, Jack and

Katherine remain sheer gold; and Phyllis, Ashley, Nick, Sharon, Billy, Victoria, Michael, Lauren, Neil, Jill, Kevin, Chloe,
Gloria, etc. rotate in and out of story beautifully.

Cons: Y&R is becoming a bit of a graveyard for cast-off stars
from other shows. Big names like Stephen Nichols (ex-Patch,
"Days"), Maura West (ex-Carly, "ATWT"), Tristan Rogers
(ex-Scorpio, "GH") and now the biggest get of them all Genie
Francis (duh Laura, "GH"; see also: the cover!) now toil in
Genoa City – where there wasn't a lot of room to begin with.
If they take airtime from snoozy Malcolm, Abby and her
nakedness, or any more Sheila/Lauren/Patty doppelgangers,
it's fine. If they usurp Phyllis, Billy or Ashley, that's going to
be trouble.

Prognosis: Excellent.

Suggested Improvements: More big, splashy events. And
I realize that magazine writers are probably the only ones
bothered by the printing schedule of Billy's magazine "Restless Style," but when Phyllis writes an article on Tuesday, it

hits the stands Wednesday, and they get the sales figures on Thursday, my head explodes.

THE BOLD AND THE BEAUTIFUL

Pros: Has won the Emmy for Best Show the last three years. Bradley Bell, protégé and son of William J. Bell, is head writer and executive producer of this show, which is the #1 soap opera in the world and airs in over 100 countries. Brad could drive story with just his four original actors - John McCook (Eric), Susan Flannery (Stephanie), Ronn Moss (Ridge) and Katherine Kelly Lang (Brooke) – on every episode, but has layered in an effective second generation. He is also the only boss who recognizes quickly what stories are not working and dumps them immediately. It's a little jarring sometimes, but that's better than watching Donna Logan divorce Eric, reunite with her wooden high school boyfriend and then embrace the sudden child she gave birth to, lied about, and gave away. That engagement and wedding lasted a week, which was just about right.

Cons: Too many of the youth stories involve young girls "catching" men. Steffy and Hope are gorgeous and, more importantly, rich Forrester progeny. They should not come unglued when a boy doesn't like them back. Amber's retread of getting pregnant to trap a guy into marriage didn't work ten years ago with Rick Forrester, and it won't work now with Liam Spencer. And it's not nearly as interesting this time around without African-American Raymond (played by Usher – yes, that Usher) in the "Who's the daddy?" mix.

Prognosis: The best of all. "B&B's" 22-minute format lends itself to continued worldwide broadcast, and foreign interest in LA and its crazy/pretty and pretty/crazy people guarantees that the money will just keep rolling in. You haven't lived until you've watched "B&B," which is called "Beautiful" in Italy and airs in prime time, dubbed into Italian. How do you say "catfight" in the language of love?

Suggested Improvements: "GH" has had an acting coach named John Homa on set for 15 years. Since "B&B" repeatedly hires gorgeous but very green young actors, a skilled acting coach on set would be a wise investment. And let Heather Tom (Katie) and Jack Wagner (Nick) act!

Taking all of this into account, even the silliest scene on every soap is better than 90% of what currently airs on Daytime Television. And it's delicious fodder for fans on the web to chew up and spit out, which is something they will never do with judge shows, game shows or talk shows – especially not now with Oprah gone.

Yes, sometimes you get a spotty actor with a shaved torso wooing a girl with three personalities, but even then… soaps *matter*.

CHAPTER 16

The Heart of the Matter

"Bring in the bottled lightning, a clean tumbler, and a corkscrew."
- Charles Dickens

It was Irna Phillips who figured out how to shape Dickens' dramatic lightning into a radio show that millions of women tuned into every day. She did it again when soaps moved to television, using the cliffhanger, the tag, the dramatic music; every convention we love about soaps to bring them to life. She brought the characters into our homes and our hearts, hooking us with their daily foibles and their continued insistence that tomorrow would be better.

That tomorrow *will* be better.

PASSION

No matter how difficult a soap character's life is, they always look forward to the next day being better and brighter. The way they rise up every day to face each new challenge is inspiring.

"People count on soaps for entertainment and escapism," asserts Thorsten Kaye. "Their show changes their day. Soaps make an emotional impact on a huge amount of people every day. That's important. That *matters*."

In the exact same way that sports matter to their legion of fans.

"Sports are a great analogy," offers "OLTL" Executive Producer Frank Valentini, "because in the same way that men traditionally talked about sports, women talked about soaps. They both discussed the players and the outcomes. 'Did you see what Erica did today? Can you believe what B&B is doing?' Just as baseball is a national pastime, so are soap operas."

Baseball has weathered steroid scandals and inflated ticket prices and lower TV ratings, yet no one ever talks about canceling baseball. Soaps have weathered far less turmoil, yet their future is uncertain. The devotion people feel for their sports team is exactly the same as the passion they feel for their soap. It's a rare connection that should be nurtured and treasured.

A home run.

THE NUMBERS ARE THERE

How is "Bethenny Ever After" a hit on Bravo with one million viewers, while "One Life to Live" is canceled with three times that many people watching?

A few weeks after ABC announced it was replacing "OLTL" with a weight loss show (insert gag joke here), "OLTL" boasted a week over week gain of 263,000 viewers, and a year over year gain of 507,000 viewers. There were almost 2.8 million people watching every day, and that's just the viewers who are *actually being counted*. ABC never got a true measure of the people, demos, or loyalty towards their soaps, because their viewers were diluted across four showings daily on SOAPnet (which didn't count), weekend marathons (which didn't count) and viewers watching the ABC air show on DVR the next day or later (which didn't count). Who sits in a conference room at ABC and says, "Oprah and Regis are leaving daytime after 25 years, so let's take Erica Kane and Viki Buchanan away, too!"

Daytime isn't dying, it's being murdered.

A show that jumped half a million viewers year over year with no support or promotion from the network deserves a closer look. The numbers are still there – make them work! Millions of rabid, loyal fans will follow their shows anywhere (as proven by SOAPnet), so where is the creative thinking towards a business model that could work economically? I outlined a series of ideas earlier, and I'm not even a network exec. How are none of these solutions even considered before pulling the plug on an 80 year-old proven, beloved genre?

Since ABC is just seeing this as a business, surely they appreciate the quality of the soap audience. The level of engagement with the programming and the loyalty are huge selling points to an advertiser. Aren't those the viewers they want to reach, rather than someone flipping through a food show?

Write to the network execs, saying you watch ABC, NBC or CBS for your soap opera every day. (You can Google the names and addresses.) Tell the top execs that your soap is a DESTINATION for you, unlike any of the talk shows, game shows, judge shows or reality shows on their networks. If you are under 48, include your age. If you're not, lie! (Just because you're outside the age range of what some exec has decided is "meaningful," doesn't mean you don't BUY STUFF.)

The time to act is now - because as any fan of "Another World," "Guiding Light," "As The World Turns," "Santa Barbara," "Passions," the list goes on… will tell you, once a soap is canceled it's too late. They sell the clothes, furniture, wedding chapels and jail cells, and they turn off the lights.

The only time a character is ever really dead is when a soap goes off the air.

SOCIAL ISSUES

When people describe soaps as "a women's medium," there could be no higher compliment. Irna Phillips invented the soap opera form of storytelling in 1930, meaning a woman is responsible for the billions of dollars earned by the networks, companies, and millions of employees who have worked on them in the 81 years since. I mean, ten years before that, women couldn't even vote in the U.S. and here comes this "spinster" able to re-imagine Scheherazade's story of *A Thousand and One Nights* into a serial format for radio so she can sell soap to stay-at-home moms.

Think about that. In the ancient tale of Scheherazade, a beauty married a Sultan with the distasteful habit of marrying a virgin at night and killing her in the morning. The well-educated Scheherazade stayed alive by concocting tales for her cranky husband, but not finishing them. At the end of one thousand and one nights, Scheherazade took a chance and told the King she had no more stories for him. Lucky for her, the King had fallen in love with his clever bride and her crazy stories. He not only spared her life, he made her his Queen.

It's not quite Irna Phillips' life story, but it's just as dramatic.

"There is a destiny that makes us brothers," quoted Irna on "The Guiding Light's" first radio broadcast in 1937. "None goes his way alone. All that we send into the lives of others, comes back into our own."

That is certainly true of the thousands of social issue stories Irna pioneered that soaps have told over the years, entertaining the audience while educating them at the same time. How many women are alive today because Monica Quartermaine, Viki Buchanan and Lillian Raines got breast cancer and taught viewers about early detection? Who even knew what a Pap Test was before Bert Bauer had one in 1962, and caught her uterine cancer?

Soaps break down stereotypes by bringing people of all ages and colors into your home every day. I doubt my Iowa-born grandmother would have been so accepting of a white man and black woman getting married if she hadn't had the chance to watch Duncan and Jessica fall so deeply in love on "As The World Turns" first. They were the first interracial couple she "knew."

You may not personally know a kid being bullied, but it will break your heart to watch "OLTL's" asthmatic Shane have his inhaler stolen while being called "Weezie." It will also educate you. Soaps have been groundbreaking since day one, and their relevance to American women cannot be underestimated.

CONNECTION

"Soaps are like watching 'Old Faithful,'" praises famed novelist Peter Straub. "All these plots come leaping out at you. That keeps things whizzing along at a great pace, providing an immense amount of interest and feeling."

And comfort. There is great solace in knowing that the people you have grown to love will be in your living room again tomorrow.

"Stories unfold into other stories, leaving bits of them on the side of the road," notes Straub. "But it doesn't matter, because the internal heart is going to roll on in a new direction. That's a very exciting idea. It has to do with boundaryless excess; a lack of containment on soaps. They operate as dreams, completely poker-faced. I think that is breathtaking. Soap operas may be our truest source of luxury in narrative."

Indeed, you never know what you're going to get from day to day, but you know that something important will happen to someone you care about, and that that person will probably look very beautiful when it does.

"They are a surefire, faithful source of sheer, innocent, narrative pleasure," Straub says with a smile. "I don't see why anyone would want to do away with an art form that has such marvelous qualities as that."

How can we keep our soaps on the air?

"Make them compulsory," quips Straub. "And I would do the same with Jazz."

"Soaps are unlike any other form of television because the audience feels what the character feels," offers Y&R's Michelle Stafford (Phyllis). "They're on the ride with you. If someone is going through a divorce and the writer is telling the history of this woman's personal pain - and the actor is good enough to portray it in realistic manner - that audience member says, 'This is how I feel.' It gives them comfort. Or, it makes them angry and gets them to be stronger in their life."

Viewers identify more with soap characters than any other because we know them.

"The way soaps are written, you are in the mind of the character, thinking what they are thinking," adds Stafford. "You are completely connected to that character in your home every day. If the actor and writer have played it truthfully, it makes the audience feel. It opens them up."

Stafford knows because she got hooked as a "young tot" to the ABC soap "Ryan's Hope," which aired from 1975-1989.

"I felt very connected to the character of Delia on 'Ryan's Hope' because she was so broken. No one understood her, and she was trying so hard to be understood. All she was trying to do was fit in, and she couldn't. No one wanted her to. I loved that. I connected to that character."

The feeling of not fitting in would naturally speak to a young viewer like Stafford at the time, but she adds that struggles of all kinds speak to the audience – and actually empower them.

"I was very hooked on Karen Wolek on 'One Life To Live,'" she adds with a laugh. "Here I am - a young girl connecting to this prostitute! - but she was an underdog and she was trying to be good. A woman from the wrong side of the tracks just trying to be cared for. I have always liked characters like that. I was never interested in the typical heroine. I thought they were pretty, but they weren't as interesting to me as Delia and Karen, who were also played by two great actresses [Ilene Kristen and Judith Light]."

Stafford liked them so much, she grew up to be one of them.

This pure devotion exists only between a soap opera and its fans. And the networks need to do everything possible to save this golden art form – now.

FAMILY

The strong connection between soaps and their viewers creates a sense of family like no other form of entertainment. We *know* these people. We rely on them to be there for us through good and bad, just as we are there for them through good (splashy weddings) and bad (murder trials). The rhythm and routine of a soap is much like that of baseball, which has always kept this country going through tough times. Our soaps keep us going. Their constant nature is comforting, as is the sense of community that soap fans are all a part of.

There is great solace in knowing that you can turn on "Days of our Lives" and watch the Hortons decorate the

Christmas tree, reminiscing about each ornament and the loved one it represents. Even Macdonald Carey's voice in the opening credits every day is soothing.

"Like sands through the hour glass…"

Fans of the shows that have ended don't have the chance to check back in on faves like Josh and Reva, Lily and Holden, Mason and Julia, Alex and Ava, Ethan and Theresa, or the hundreds of other characters and couples we have loved and lost.

Personally, I picture them doing all the things we loved to watch: fighting, making up, being all lovey-dovey and then doing it again. Example: Holden and Lily (Martha Byrne) make up by sneaking off to the Snyder Pond for a little romance where they run into Jack and Carly having a picnic with their new baby. Try it!

It's the same way I picture my childhood corgi running free on a farm upstate.

LOVE

Soap operas matter in the same way playing with that childhood pet mattered… coming downstairs to see what

Santa brought on Christmas morning… going back to your old high school and thanking your favorite teacher… kissing your first boyfriend… watching your child graduate… smelling a baby… hugging an old friend. Soaps are that old friend. They visit every day, their "internal heart" beating to the delight of passionate fans who tune in daily for that hug. They are the books that never end, the friend that won't let you down, the daily hug you can count on. Their fans will make sure of it.

"Soaps fulfill the fantasy of family, and the fantasy of love," sums up Frank Valentini. "On soaps, the person you love will always be there for you, and they will always be forgiving. You can follow your heart, because you will always be loved by your family, your friends, and the love of your life. Who wouldn't want that?"

Who, indeed.

The mother of the American soap opera, Irna Phillips.

Ed Bryce, Charita Bauer, Robert Gentry and Theo Getz made up GL's Bauer family in the 1950s.

Note that this early ATWT cast photo was "signed" by the characters, not the actors, and was given away "Compliments of Cheers."

REGULAR DAY

BLOCKING & RUN THRU	11:15 - 1:15
BREAK & NOTES	1:15 - 1:30
DRESS	1:30 - 2:00
BREAK & NOTES	2:00 - 2:30
TAPE	2:30 - 3:00

DOUBLE TAPE DAY

BLOCKING & RUN THRU	10:15 - 12:15
BREAK & NOTES	12:15 - 12:30
DRESS	12:30 - 1:00
BREAK & NOTES	1:00 - 1:30
TAPE (SHOW #1)	1:30 - 2:00
LUNCH	2:00 - 3:30
BLOCKING & RUN THUR	3:30 - 5:35
BREAK & NOTES	5:35 - 5:45
DRESS	5:45 - 6:15
BREAK & NOTES	6:15 - 6:45
TAPE (SHOW #2)	6:45 - 7:15

Just another "day" at "Days Of Our Lives" in the early days.

"More coffee, dear?" Nancy (Helen Wagner) asked Chris
(Don MacLaughlin) every morning on ATWT.

DAYS' Tom and Alice Horton had their hands full with their daughter…
the nun.

Y&R's Lance (John McCook) and Lorie (Jaime Lyn Bauer) spent most of their time in bed.

Jennifer (Gillian Spencer) was undone by Bob's affair with her sister Kim (Kathryn Hays) – and so were ATWT viewers.

The Hortons ruled "Days" through the 1970s:
Doug, Mickey, Laura, Bill, Julie, Alice and Tom.

This is what a bored housewife looks like: ATWT's Lisa (Eileen Fulton)
with Bob (Don Hastings).

Agnes Nixon with her favorite "vixen" Susan Lucci in January, 2010.

William J. Bell and Jeanne Cooper at the Y&R anniversary party in 2003.

Honcho Ken Corday and star Frances Reid at a DAYS anniversary party in the 1990s.

B&B's Fab Four – John McCook, Susan Flannery, Ronn Moss and Katherine Kelly Lang – on location in Lake Como, Italy.

Reva (Kim Zimmer) and Josh (Robert Newman) faced the future together in GL's last scene.

Y&R's Phyllis (Michelle Stafford) and Nick (Joshua Morrow) were the couch sex champions in 2010.

Every time B&B's Ridge and Brooke tie the knot, it's "forever."

Peter Reckell and Kristian Alfonso have played passionate lovers Bo and Hope on DAYS for almost 30 years, despite not always getting along.

*ATWT's Martha Byrne (Lily) fixed up her onscreen husband Jon Hensley
(Holden) with his real-life wife Kelley.*

*ATWT's Eileen Fulton invented the famous "Granny Clause" in her
contract.*

Only on soaps would Y&R's Skye and Sharon have a catfight on top of a volcano.

B&B's Brooke and Thomas washed up on an island in strategically torn clothing.

Christopher Walken (left, who was then known as Glen Walken), played GL's young Mike Bauer (pictured with Charita Bauer and Lyle Sudrow).

Brock (Beau Kazer) lent an ear to Snapper (David Hasselhoff) in the early days of Y&R.

Julianne Moore returned to her soap roots to play Frannie on ATWT near the show's end (with Helen Wagner and Eileen Fulton).

AMC's Angie (Debbi Morgan) and Jesse (Darnell Williams) are daytime's reigning black couple.

AMC's Susan Lucci and Eden Riegel at the Emmys after a strong Erica/Bianca year.

OLTL's Scott Evans and Brett Claywell at the 2010 GLAAD media awards.

GH's Maurice Benard (Sonny) and his wife, Paula, have been open about his manic depression.

B&B's Stephanie and Brooke met Dayzee (left) at an LA homeless shelter.

Kelly Ripa and Mark Consuelos are married 15 years and still going strong.

ATWT scribe and hero, Doug Marland.

GL's Ellen Wheeler (right) directed Gina Tognoni (Dinah, left) to wear a giant parka in Peapack.

Cady McClain won a 2004 Emmy, but it wasn't enough to keep AMC from poisoning her with pancakes.

Why didn't GL use bigger soap for product placement in this scene with Frank and Harley?

GH's Sonny (Maurice Benard) and Jason (Steve Burton) remain the dreamiest mobsters to ever hit Daytime.

*OLTL Executive Producer Frank Valentini directs his
biggest star, Erika Slezak (Viki).*

*Zach (Thorsten Kaye) and Kendall (Alicia Minshew) were AMC's money
couple – so naturally they "killed" him in a plane crash.*

Photo Credits

CPSIA information can be obtained at www.ICGtesting.com
Printed in the USA
237059LV00002B/12/P